ALSO BY BETSY LERNER

The Forest for the Trees

food AND loathing

a Lament

Betsy Lerner

SIMON & SCHUSTER

New York   London   Toronto   Sydney   Singapore

SIMON & SCHUSTER
Rockefeller Center
1230 Avenue of the Americas
New York, NY 10020

SIMON & SCHUSTER and colophon are registered trademarks
of Simon & Schuster, Inc.

For information regarding special discounts for bulk purchases,
please contact Simon & Schuster Special Sales:
1-800-456-6798 or business@simonandschuster.com

Designed by Jan Pisciotta

The names and characteristics of some individuals
in this book have been changed.

Manufactured in the United States of America

1 3 5 7 9 10 8 6 4 2

Library of Congress Cataloging-in-Publication Data

Lerner, Betsy.
Food and loathing : a lament / Betsy Lerner.
p. cm.
1. Lerner, Betsy—Health. 2. Eating disorders—Patients—Biography.
3. Compulsive eating—Anecdotes. 4. Weight loss. I. Title.

RC552.E18 L47 2003
362.2'7—dc21   2002030220

ISBN 0-7432-2183-4

For John

Of course I believe in free will.
What choice do I have?

—I. B. Singer

Contents

food AND loathing

One

You Should Feel Lucky

It is 1972. I am twelve years old. It is the first day of sixth grade, and I am standing in the girls' gymnasium waiting to be weighed. My last name begins with L, so I am exactly in the middle of the line. The thinnest girl in class stands directly in front of me. At the front of the line, our gym teacher, Miss Match, with her butch haircut, slim boy hips, and two-pack-a-day gravelly voice, barks out our names. Looming beside her is that gray piece of metal: the scale. Miss Match weighs each girl and calls out the number for her assistant coach to record on her clipboard. Her assistant jots the numbers with her ballpoint pen: 100, 105, 88, 120. The line moves forward and I begin to sweat. The girl ahead of me has arms and legs like twigs. Her thighs swim inside her gym shorts. She is blond and has huge, soulful eyes. In seventh grade she will become my best friend, but for now she is this skinny thing and I hate her. Three girls behind is my current best friend, Anna Mankowicz, who has shot up over the last year to a sinewy five foot six. She towers over us and has bona fide breasts. I also know that she has hair down there. I love her, but I am also afraid of her, of her recent developments. Boys like her.

A few girls behind Anna is Wanda Mueller. She is not my friend or anyone else's. The reason is obvious: she's the fattest girl in the class. She's really, really big. Tall *and* fat. She usually wears skirts, and her legs look like telephone poles that dead-end at her sensible brown shoes. Her cheeks flush quickly and are often either firing up or fading out. For me, she is the safety net. She's the one everyone picks on, the one who gets ostracized. She protects me from the same fate.

Even at age twelve, I have developed an elaborate set of coping mechanisms to keep people from teasing me. They include being funny and being nice and behaving in such a fashion that everyone in the world will like me.

You Should Feel Lucky

Maintaining this facade takes a great deal of energy, since I am filled with self-loathing and a good dollop of misanthropy. Still, I am able to hide my outsized feelings because the desire to be liked and not ridiculed is stronger than all the hatred I can conjure. I have always been able to befriend my deepest enemy and thus keep him—or her—from hurting me. In the sixth grade, hurting people took the form of name-calling: fag, fairy, wimp, fat. When I read a purloined copy of *The Godfather* that was making the rounds through our sixth-grade class, mostly for the sex scenes, I found instead Vito Corleone's famous line, "Keep your friends close but your enemies closer." I kept his counsel, for I knew exactly what he meant. By the time I reached the sixth grade, I couldn't stand most of my closest friends.

∞

The line moves up. I hate the way my gym shorts cling to my skin. It's a one-piece rayon suit, and its goal in life is to cling and ride up my ass. The line continues. I start to panic. I tell myself, *I'm not Wanda Mueller. At least I'm not Wanda.* Then I feel guilty. I think about lunch and how my mother always packs the same thing: an egg salad or tuna fish sandwich and a piece of fruit. Never a cookie or a sweet. No little bags of potato chips or Fritos. *Too fatten-*

ing. I hate Miss Match. She's been known to make remarks about weight, and though she's never directed one at me, I live in terror that she might. The skinny flower in front of me steps up to the scale. Match slides the balance to the left, lower and lower. Finally, she calls out, "seventy-eight." That's what I weighed in the third grade, for Chrissake.

My face is grim as I step up. I watch Miss Match's knuckly fingers work the balance toward the upper end of the scale in five-pound increments. It takes forever. This slow torture, I am certain, is deliberate. On that day of my twelfth year, I weighed 134. I was five feet tall. It was too much. *What I would give to see that number again.*

After school, and much cajoling, Anna Mankowicz's mother agrees to take us to Dunkin' Donuts as a back-to-school treat. We live in a suburb of New Haven and have to drive the fifteen or so minutes into town, down Whalley Avenue, a main thoroughfare that is home to most of my favorite fast-food chains. I sit in the back seat with Anna while her two younger brothers maul each other in the way-back of the station wagon. Anna's brothers are big guys, destined to play all manner of contact sports.

You Should Feel Lucky

Anna's mother is petite. She secures her frosted hair beneath a velvet navy blue hair band. She wears culottes and a polo shirt and always looks as if she is coming off the golf course triumphant after sinking a difficult putt. I am afraid of her, though I have no reason to be. I sense that she can be mean.

At the doughnut counter, Anna and I ask for our usual: glazed. The boys scarf down crullers. Mrs. Mankowicz sips at her black coffee. We are happily eating our doughnuts when the youngest, a strapping boy nearly six feet tall, announces he wants another. His brother chimes in that he does, too, and Anna follows suit. I keep silent, not because I don't want another—those glazed things are like air—but because I am afraid the request might appear rude. After all, I am not a member of the family. I know Mrs. Mankowicz is going to treat me, but I am anxious about presuming the lengths of her generosity. Too, my silence shelters a deeper fear: I am afraid of looking like a pig. I already feel self-conscious next to my svelte friend, my thighs sticking to the pink vinyl stool.

"Boys, you may choose another doughnut," Mrs. Mankowicz begins, "but Anna, I don't want you eating another. You've got a figure to watch."

I sit there frozen. I can't believe my ears. For all the

hinting and prompting and gesturing and glancing my mother does to convey her disapproval of my eating too much, she has never once come out and said "You can't eat that." She has never denied me a bite. I know that she wishes I would lose weight, disapproves when I take seconds or order something fattening at a restaurant, but she never uses her authority as my mother to limit my food intake.

"Betsy, would you like another?" Mrs. Mankowicz smiles at me, her hot pink lipstick now faded, imprinted instead on the lip of the mug before her.

I know she is being polite. But her words cut through me. If I take the doughnut, then I am admitting defeat. After all, doesn't her offer imply that my figure is beyond watching? Already too chubby, I might as well pile it on. Or I could decline the doughnut and act as if I am full. (Full? There aren't enough doughnuts in the state of Connecticut!) Mrs. Mankowicz's dark eyes are on me, waiting for my response, seeming to know that I want to eat everything in sight. I look into her eyes, trying not to cry and trying to understand if she is being cruel or if I am being too sensitive, as I am usually charged.

I am also trying to maintain a shred of dignity in front of my best friend and her two brothers, who seem oblivious to my dilemma. Mrs. Mankowicz is waiting. It is a simple question: Do I or do I not want another doughnut? Reinterpreted, however, through the web of self-loathing known as my inner life, it sounds more like: Do you want to die by lethal injection or the electric chair?

By now the boys have nearly finished their seconds. I want to kill Anna's mother. I want to rip every pink thing from this shit-box of a doughnut shop and smear it with chocolate custard. I want to scream in her tight little face: *You know I want another doughnut, you fucking bitch.* But more than anything, I want to race home to my mother and lambaste her for letting me feed my face. I want her to control me the way Mrs. Mankowicz controls Anna, so I can be beautiful and slim. I want to throttle my mother for letting this happen to me. But then I pull myself together. I tell myself that I am happy I have my mother and not this controlling bitch. I am happy that my mother doesn't tell me what to eat. I am happy because I am my own person and I will deal with my weight in my own way. Who would want a mother like that, anyway?

"No, thank you," I say. "I'm not hungry."

food and loathing

The following year, Anna went to private school and I attended public school in our suburb. We continued to see each other at our temple for the final year of Hebrew school classes, which would culminate in our being bas mitzvahed. Our circle hated Hebrew school and felt that the required two afternoons a week were a waste of time. In our religious ennui, we regularly gathered in the woods behind the school to play truth or dare and smoke cigarettes.

The game required players to either make good on a dare or answer any question truthfully. The questions we asked were aimed to humiliate and were usually about sex, attempting to determine how much experience each of us had had. Since we were all completely inexperienced, the game became one of bluffing. Once Reva, the skinny girl from gym class, was asked if she swallowed or spit it out. After searching our faces for a clue, she blurted: "Spit *what* out?" The boys broke up in guffaws. And when my friend looked at me, I made a superior, sorry face as if I knew the answer.

It all sounds innocent enough, but as we pushed each other further and further, waiting to see who would crack, it became an unrelenting game of chicken. Uptight about my body and convinced that my inexperience with boys was related, I found the game agonizing. But beyond the social politics of our little game, something else was becoming clear: all the boys were in love with Anna. And the alpha male of our group, Petey Marks, was clearly ready to claim her for his own.

I watched all this happen with the silent eye of the documentarian. Anna's marvelous neck tilting backward as she laughed too hard at his jokes. Petey lighting two cigarettes in his mouth and handing one off to her. How I longed for him to lift a cigarette from his mouth and hand it to me. Instead, when I asked him for a light, he'd whip his lighter in my direction with a dismissive flick. *Light it yourself.* I marveled at the sinew behind Anna's knees and the long, olive-colored thighs that disappeared into her cotton shorts. How easily she could pop up from sitting cross-legged, all in one motion, while I struggled to haul myself up. In class I coveted the way she double-crossed her legs beneath her desk, while I could barely cross one chubby thigh over the other.

In the woods, I watched Anna and Petey go from teasing to wrestling to making out. I watched how a girl would captivate a guy and he would circle his wagons around her. To me, she denied even liking him, afraid she would hurt me. But her protection was too close to condescension, or worse, pity. I swore from that time forward I would never let a girlfriend think I cared for a moment when she canceled plans with me and waltzed off with her new beau. As for Anna, deny it as she might, I knew her tongue and mouth had already found his, and I knew that it was only a matter of time till they went further.

Had it been only a year earlier when Anna played make-out with me? When she would pounce on me as we watched our favorite soap opera, *General Hospital,* pretending to be Luke and Laura, and kiss me wildly with her hand sealed over my mouth, her spacious hips grinding into mine. Though we were always fully dressed, I didn't play these make-out games with anyone else, and I felt an illicit thrill of collusion. But now, behind B'nai Jacob, I watched my best friend disappear deeper into the woods, and I knew I had lost her forever. By thirteen I considered myself something of an expert on human behavior, and I understood that in the poker game of life, boyfriend trumps best friend.

In junior high I encountered a new paradigm for thinking about myself, in the form of a laminated chart that our science teacher pulled out—a diagram outlining the three body types: ectomorph, mesomorph, and endomorph. *Here it comes,* I thought. We're going to have to identify ourselves by body type, and I am going to be standing alone with Wanda Mueller and the one fat boy in our class. I glanced at Wanda a few rows behind and was sickened to see her clotted cheeks.

Hitting the chart with her rubber-tipped pointer, the science teacher recited a little trick to remember the types: the ectomorph eats to live, the mesomorph eats and lives, and the endomorph lives to eat. This information hit me with a number of terrifying simultaneous thoughts: Did I live *to* eat? Was the act of stuffing my face my raison d'être? I had already developed some sneak-eating habits, and I was highly aware of how much everyone else was eating. By now the world of food had been precisely divided into two camps: the dietetic and the forbidden. Was it possible that the act of filling my mouth was the only thing that brought me real pleasure? What was I feeling when I watched Petey and Anna's lips seal? Of all those beautiful best friends, first Anna, then Reva, would I love any as well as my most reliable and trusted friend, food?

When puberty kicked in and the rest of the known world at Amity Junior High paired off, I protected myself by befriending all the boys who weren't interested in dating me. If I had a slight crush on a fellow, I'd immediately fix him up with a prettier, thinner girl, then privately bemoan my outcast state. I prided myself on being the only girl allowed in the boy's poker game in study hall. Being friends with the coolest guys offered some protection, some consolation, though I would much rather have held hands than dealt them.

To all outward appearances, I was a bright girl who got excellent grades. I made people laugh. I was good at lots of creative things, like making pottery, and I was starting to write poems. I had lots of friends. I was funny, I was generous, I was reliable. Though I didn't know it at the time, I was becoming your standard-issue fat friend.

I didn't really know how I looked. In part, I kept my body hidden even from myself, adopting the standard garb of adolescent angst: fatigues, flannel shirts, sneakers without socks. I'd wear batik or Indian-print wraparound skirts and clogs when I had to get dressed up. I kept my hair long, past my shoulders, and never pulled it back, as my mother would have liked. But I relied on more than loose clothes and hair to camouflage my weight. I used every fiber of my personality to keep a person from thinking I was fat. When I looked in the mirror I saw that my face was pudgy, no cheekbones in evidence. I had hazel eyes, a small nose from my father's side, and thick, wavy, brown hair. I wasn't happy with my reflection, yet I suspected that if I ever lost weight, boys might actually consider me pretty.

Only one thing was holding me back. As my mother would occasionally croon, "If you were thin, you'd be perfect." She meant it as a compliment; the sad truth is, I believed it. I really thought the only thing between me and perfection was thirty pounds.

$$\infty$$

My mother was neither heavy nor thin, and like most women, she constantly monitored her waistline. She dressed to hide problem areas rather than show off, preferring tailored clothes to frills, flannel pajamas to silky nightgowns, sensible, well-fitting pumps to anything strappy and sexy. My mom didn't have great gams or a fabulous bottom, and if she had she probably wouldn't have emphasized them, as many women do. It simply wasn't her style to call attention to herself.

I would scrutinize her as she performed her rituals of hair and makeup, the routine of creams and powders, liners and lipsticks. But my mother never seemed to take any pleasure in getting dressed up. She put on makeup as if following a recipe. She was always too rough, rubbing in foundation as if she wanted to erase her own cheek, nearly smacking herself with the powder puff. Her hair took the worst beating. She would whack the brush at the side of her head to shape her short, tight curls into a reasonable helmet.

My mother believed she was plain, but she considered herself an expert at "maximizing her looks." It was she who tutored me in the art of camouflage. She knew which styles were slenderizing and lengthening. She knew exactly how long a hem or sleeve should be, what should be tucked in, what tucked out. She knew about belts and bags and matching accessories. My mother insisted that certain types of clothes—turtlenecks, double-breasted jackets, pleats—were disastrous for me. She liked a short jacket on me; I preferred long. And she liked bright, strong colors, which became a sore point later, when I left home for college in New York City, a town that basically required only one thing of you: that you wear black.

My mother tried desperately to get me to wear "good" clothes, sporty combinations. I can still see the frightened faces of the saleswomen, whose initially hopeful and helpful demeanor shrank in the face of my obstinacy. My mother was always extremely solicitous of these women, whose pancake makeup came to an abrupt end in a masklike line at their jaw, whose pill-y cardigans smelled of mothballs, whose bifocals hung from a strand of shiny beads like a necklace, resting on their bosom shelves.

"Excuse me," she'd say to one of these women. "Can you show us the latest styles?"

I would rush away, horrified that my own mother thought a geriatric saleswoman with more lipstick on her teeth than on her lips could know what would look good on me. I couldn't stand it when they ran their eyes over my body, dressing me like some plus-size cutout doll. When I'd return with a handful of dark things, the dressing room would be filled with mix-and-match separates, my mother unzipping skirts and pants, eager for me to try them on.

"I can't believe you think I'd wear that," I'd spit.

"Betsy, just try it. It's the cut that matters. You don't know if it's a flattering cut until you try."

My mother believed in the right cuts and good lines and well-made clothes as an antidote to bodies that were less well cut. I should have been grateful for her generosity and tenacity, but as each article of clothing failed to zip up my backside, I'd attack her choice.

"That's disgusting," I'd sneer, as if she, too, were disgusting. "You're ruining my life."

My mother would finally retreat, realizing that I wasn't going to come around. She never yelled—on the contrary, she avoided making a scene at all costs. Sometimes the saleslady would peek in to see if we needed a different size. My mother would shrug a defeated thank-you, her face trying to offer the catch-all explanation: *teenager.* And as the saleswoman retreated, I'd feel victorious, but only for a moment. Watching my mother sadly zip and fold the clothes I'd rejected, her eyes avoiding mine, I understood that everything about the scene was wrong. I hadn't been honest with myself at Dunkin' Donuts. I did want my mother to stop me.

As if to make me feel better, my mother often pointed out people with infirmities—a girl pulling her polio-ridden body along with crutches, a man with a club foot—always making the same point: thank god you have something you can change. *Pooh-pooh-pooh,* she would rush to say following one of these sightings, *god forbid, you shouldn't know from it.* Fate would surely throw a cold eye on us for thinking such thoughts, for comparing ourselves to those less fortunate.

Each year at Yom Kippur services we waited in shul to see which of the latest fashions Mrs. Slotkin would show up in. A woman with unspeakably beaked features (her nose and fingernails curled in a way that frightened me as a child), she nonetheless paraded "like a beauty queen," to use my mother's words, up and down the aisle in quilted suits and perfectly matching accessories. Her liquid eyeliner made her look like Snow White's stepmother, and even in adult memory, Mrs. Slotkin appears to me as the evil queen herself.

My mother and I endlessly debated what this revealed about Mrs. Slotkin's inner life. Did she doll herself up because she thought she was the living end? Or was it because she suffered, as we did, from low self-esteem? Did she even have an inner life? What would the rabbis say? Yom Kippur services were nothing if not a day at the schadenfreude races. We clicked and clucked among ourselves about this one's divorce and that one's cancer, who had lost weight and who was bigger than ever. I often wondered what it said about our own inner lives as we sat there silently condemning half the congregation on the very day we were meant to atone. As the T-shirt slogan goes, thank god we were atheists.

∞

One afternoon after Hebrew school, my mother told me she didn't believe in god. My head was in the fridge when I asked her. She was facing the wall as she ironed a stack of my father's shirts. I didn't have to watch to know that she was methodically applying the iron first to each sleeve, then the back, then the front panels. When I closed the door of the refrigerator, she was snaking the tip of the iron around the buttons. She stopped for a moment, looked up at the ceiling as if to check one last time, then shook her head, no.

"Why not?" I asked, surprised by her answer.

"Because of Barbara," she said. I knew I had a sister who had died. I was four at the time and she was two. I knew it was a terrible thing, but since my parents banished all pictures of her and never, not once, mentioned her, I thought they had forgotten about her, as I had. My older sister and I didn't go to the funeral. And my younger sister, who was born six years after the tragedy, didn't even know about her. In a way, for me, she didn't die so much as cease to exist.

"You still think about her?" I asked. The minute I asked I knew it was a stupid question.

"All the time," she said, and slipped the freshly pressed shirt onto a hanger.

I took my cheese and apple and plopped down in front of the TV. The familiar *Brady Bunch* theme music came on. I had seen every episode at least three times, but I sat there in my usual after-school stupor, watching the repeat. How was it possible that she thought of my sister all the time? The only time I really thought about Barbara was when I encountered the plaque commemorating her death in a long, dark corridor of our temple.

I was in the third grade, and my girlfriends and I weren't supposed to be in that hall where the plaques were hung, outside the sanctuary. But the highly polished linoleum floors beckoned, and we found ourselves surfing the halls in our socks after Hebrew school. The wall of plaques, with its tiny orange lights glowing across the surface, looked like a giant switchboard. Reading the names on some of the plaques, we giggled at how old-fashioned they sounded: Izzy, Doris, Ida. And then I saw her name: Barbara B. Lerner November 20, 1964. Of course I knew who she was, but, faced with the plaque, I saw the potential for drama. I pointed it out to my friends. Their faces registered bewilderment at first. They continued to scrutinize the plaque until it dawned on them that Barbara must have been my little sister. I looked at them and back at the wall as if to say: *All that's left of a two-year-old girl is in that cold brass plaque.*

None of us had ever dared touch the Wall of the Dead. But now I moved my hand to that little bulb next to my sister's name, closed my eyes, and twisted it on. I stood there with my hand clasped around the bulb, my hand turning a devilish orange from the light within, staring at my friends with an expression somewhere between defiance and possession. They started crying like the possessed girls in *The Crucible,* each infecting the other with hysteria. The more they reacted, the more stoic I became. I didn't feel any sorrow for the loss of my sister; instead I basked in the gravity of their attention, as if having a sister who died made me more important. I knew even then that my bid for attention was craven. Even if I was too young to understand the enormity of the tragedy, I knew better than to use her death to call attention to myself.

I've told this story to various shrinks over the years. It seemed highly symbolic—one of those key stories in the pantheon that you drag out in hopes of some enlightenment. I hoped to have an *Ordinary People* moment, like the one between Judd Hirsch and Timothy Hutton, in which Hutton recalls the tragic sailing accident when he let go of his brother's hand. He is guilt-ridden over letting his brother die, and his guilt leads to a suicide attempt. But reliving the scene in therapy with Hirsch, Hutton understands that he didn't let go so much as hold on. He dissolves in tears, finally able to mourn the loss of his brother and forgive himself for living. His therapist embraces him, and we are meant to understand the moment as cathartic.

You Should Feel Lucky

As much as I attacked the movie for being pat and simplistic, I could not stop thinking about it. After all, wasn't Mary Tyler Moore a WASP version of my own mother, coolly holding herself together through her exquisite grief? And, though I considered the casting of Judd Hirsch as the shrink the worst kind of stereotyping, didn't I long for a bear of a therapist who would help me understand what I could never quite put together? For years, I railed against *Ordinary People* and its phony portrayal of therapy, never admitting how I desperately longed for that hug. But life never offers up such Hollywood endings, epiphanies that change everything for once and for all. I never had a catharsis in twenty-odd years of therapy. I never had a shrink who hugged me.

Eventually I would forgive myself for living. Losing thirty pounds was another story.

My mother never stopped trying to convert me, pointing out heavy women who made themselves up beautifully and wore stunning outfits. Why not wear a little makeup, maximize my looks? My mother had no idea how desperate I was to look good, to lose the weight. I had already counted myself out as a person who would ever find love or happiness in this world. I knew which girls the boys liked. I could see where I was headed—the land of no boyfriends, no prom dates, no dreamy first kisses.

"You don't have a figure," my mother would sometimes say. "You have a shape." And then, to make me feel better, she'd remind me how lucky I was. "You know, some girls are pear-shaped, with those enormous hips, and some are huge on top. You're evenly distributed. You're a little chubby all over. You should feel lucky."

I knew my mother was right. I should consider myself fortunate: I *could* lose weight. But as each Monday failed to become the first day of the rest of my life, I came to believe that my failure of will was a measure of my entire character. I chalked up every indignity to this one great weakness. And I was hypersensitive to any situation that called attention to it. When the elderly salesman at our local shoestore measured my foot, never failing to expound on my extra-wide width, I wanted to strangle him with the cord that hung around his neck, dangling his shoehorn. Once I went with my father to a trade show at the New Haven Coliseum, which was set up with hundreds of mock display rooms. I ran up to one that had a piano bench and slid onto it. Without warning, the bench collapsed under my weight. We later discovered that the legs had not been screwed in, but the shame I felt as the bench gave way beneath me could have filled the Coliseum.

You Should Feel Lucky

Then there was the afternoon when a four-year-old visiting our house pointed to me and exclaimed, "She's fat." Her mother tried to hush her, which only made the child more determined to sing it from the ramparts. "She's fat, she's fat, she's fat." When I saw her as a young woman twenty years later at the Stop & Shop, where I was picking up some groceries for my mother, I ran with my cart into another aisle, my heart pounding, the shame as fresh as the day she branded me.

But the final catalyst occurred during an ordinary car ride with one of my friends. From the backseat I overheard her dad complain about his weight. "I'm up to 170," he said to his wife. "I gotta cut back." I don't remember anything else about that day, where we were going, or what else might have happened. All I knew was that at fifteen I weighed as much as a grown man. So when my mother mentioned a new kind of group for weight loss that was starting in our area, I immediately agreed to go. This was the first time she had ever brought up the subject, and under most circumstances I would have flat-out rejected any offer of help. But I was desperate. My mother told me that the group met once a week at St. Raphael's Hospital. We would be going together, my parents and I, because we all needed to lose weight. I was actually eager to start.

food and loathing

That first Thursday night, we had no idea what Overeaters Anonymous was. It was 1975 and the nation had not yet embraced the recovery movement. We didn't use terms like eating disorders, anorexia, bulimia. No attractive young feminist author had yet construed beauty as myth. Betty Friedan might have been the heart and soul of the movement, but every woman wanted to be Gloria Steinem, the hair and hips. These were the days of the grapefruit diet, the Scarsdale diet, Dexatrim, and mother's little helpers. When Lucy Ricardo had to slim down for a big performance at the Copa, she installed herself in some kind of heating box that magically melted the pounds away. The health and fitness craze hadn't hit the suburbs. Nike was still the name of a Greek goddess. Those were the days when a balanced meal included steak, when pasta was called noodles, when the only diet beverage was Tab, which came in a pink can and real men didn't drink it. When I was growing up, the only people watching their figures were us gals. Fat was not yet a feminist issue.

A dozen or so middle-aged women assembled for the meeting. Not surprisingly, my father was the only man, though he didn't seem to mind. I was the only teen and was grateful no one recognized me. The meeting was held in a cordoned-off section of the cafeteria at St.

Raphael's Hospital. The stale smell of cafeteria food hung in the air, and from behind the kitchen doors a great dishwasher hissed through its cycles. We all introduced ourselves in turn, using the same words and first names only. When it was my turn, I didn't know if I would be able to say it: *Hello, I'm Betsy. I'm a compulsive overeater.*

I have no idea how I was able to recite those words in front of my parents—and, more amazingly, to myself. Somehow I managed to swallow all the shame and pain I associated with being fat, all the chicanery I employed to conceal my food addiction, to make that simple admission. But before I could assess how it felt to admit my real identity, the room answered with a resounding: *Hello, Betsy! Welcome.*

I actually felt relief. I went home that night armed with a stack of brochures. One listed twelve questions that would help me determine if I was really a compulsive overeater; I got a perfect score. Other brochures talked about god and a Higher Power. Later for those. Two diets were offered, a "gray sheet" and an "orange sheet." The gray sheet was the more stringent program, and I opted for it. This was all or nothing: three meals a day with nothing in between. The portions were generally four ounces of protein and a half-cup of a starch. Two cups of vegetables. One fruit a day. One tablespoon of oil or one pat of butter. Just as the recovering alcoholic had to kiss all his booze goodbye and embrace sobriety, so we were expected to practice abstinence, eating only our three planned meals a day.

In just a few short months, I became not only an active member of OA, but an avid believer in the program. I followed that gray sheet to slavish perfection, started to read the Big Book from Alcoholics Anonymous, and came to believe, as the program preached, that I suffered from a disease that was cunning and baffling. My belief in and adoption of the program's tenets were absolute. Had the Hare Krishna come along instead, I'd have been dancing in saffron robes through Penn Station. So what if I didn't really get the Higher Power part? The scale was my god, and it was very happy with me. I lost eighteen pounds in the first month alone. I was on the road to perfection.

Two

My Lonely Country

The weight melted off as if I were in Lucy's magic melting box. My first ninety days flew by. Food still mattered, but now, for the first time in my life, the boundaries about what would or would not pass through my mouth became absolute. My parents were also following the diet, but they stretched the rules this way and that. I, on the other hand, was like a little Nazi. If my mother was a little worried about my rigidity, I could also see that she was thrilled with my progress. I felt her eyes on me as if I were a dress on a rack she was seriously considering.

At the meeting celebrating my first ninety days of abstinence, I received a commemorative coin and had to say a few words. I'm sure I talked about how grateful I was for my abstinence. I had easily accepted all the tenets of the program, even those beyond my ken. And I adopted all of the slogans to explain my compulsion. I believed that the desire to go off the program was "the disease talking." I believed that "the program only works if you work it." I tried to take things "one day at a time," "to live and let live." Thus armed, I had an answer for everything.

After thanking everyone for helping me achieve abstinence, I returned to my seat and overheard a woman saying matter-of-factly to her friend that I was setting myself up for a fall. She said it within earshot, with absolute certainty. In OA, it was often said that your first abstinence was a gift. It was never as easy to achieve abstinence the second time around. Any slip and you had to start over at Day One. The people celebrating anniversaries of multiple years of abstinence were treated as respected Elders of the Tribe. I heard that people could slip after months and even years. The woman who said I was heading for a fall hadn't lost any weight during the time I had been attending meetings, and I chalked up her remark to jealousy. Even my dad expressed envy at my success.

Chronically between thirty and seventy pounds overweight, my father was a classic yo-yo dieter who sampled every new diet, from Pritikin, to Scarsdale, to grapefruit and all the rest. My father and his two brothers had always struggled with weight. Family mythology has them all, as kids, working in our grandfather's candy store in Brooklyn. As the oldest, my father shouldered the most responsibility. He'd often tell us about manning the store, and I'd easily imagine him as a teenager—running the cash register, mixing an egg cream, replenishing the box of loose cigarettes, a penny apiece. I always had the impression that the three boys were left to their own devices, that the candy was theirs for the taking. My uncle Phil, the baby, fondly remembered making himself a malted whenever he was thirsty.

My father lavished us with treats: cotton candy at the circus, candy apples at the carnival, hot dogs and peanuts at the baseball game, a round tin of fancy hard candies at a Broadway show, and, best of all, popcorn and Milk Duds at the movies. I was never happier than when I was sitting beside my father at the movies in the dark, eating forbidden food. There the world was complete. I never cared how we must have looked. Feeding my face with buttery popcorn, sucking Milk Duds out of my molars, I succumbed completely to every movie I saw. I cried in torrents when Billy Jack surrendered; I could barely breathe when Ali McGraw died in *Love Story;* I was desperate to stop Mia Farrow from breaking through the closet into Ruth Gordon's apartment in *Rosemary's Baby;* I held my breath behind the headstones along with the von Trapp family as the Nazis searched the abbey.

My father had always wanted to go into "show business," and his love of theater and film and TV infected me. Once a month we'd go into New York City, where we'd visit my grandparents and see a Broadway show. At home we'd sneak off on a Wednesday night for the manager's special at the Forest, where for a dollar we would watch second-run movies in the slightly dank cavern of that theater. And every weeknight from nine to ten we had our special programs, the hour-long dramas whose names could have been substituted for the days of the week: *Ironside, Hawaii Five-O, Medical Center, Mannix, Marcus Welby, M.D.* I never understood the disparaging remarks people made about television, rejecting it as mere escapism. That was the beauty of film and TV as far as I was concerned. It was the most perfectly realized form of escape.

My Lonely Country

Walking from the hospital parking lot to the cafeteria where the OA meetings were held, I was always terrified I might see someone from my high school. If I did, my life would be over, my cover blown. When we finally got to our corner of the cafeteria, I was calmed by the familiar faces and the table displaying slightly battered pamphlets and books. Each week we began with the ritual welcome, which I never became entirely comfortable with. Sometimes the response sounded singsong to me, an irksome parrot mocking my arrival: *Hello, Betsy! Welcome.*

There was no weighing in, and talk of actual food was verboten. Each week someone was supposed to "qualify," to tell the story of how she had been ruined by food and now, thanks to the program, was in recovery. The only problem was that in our fledgling group there weren't enough people who had been in recovery long enough to qualify. To fill the gap, we often invited alcoholics from a nearby AA meeting to address our group. My parents had not made the connection between compulsive overeating and alcoholism and so did not relate to most of these speakers. I, however, was thrilled when a bona fide alcoholic joined us. They all seemed very cool, with their chain-smoking and world-weary attitudes. They weren't like my parents or my parents' friends. They didn't make small talk and keep everything polite. Rather, they told us the worst things they had ever done. In fact, they seemed to revel in the details of their dissolution. They talked about having a love affair with alcohol and about the losses that the love affair incurred: loss of family, friends, jobs, stature, self-esteem, and, finally, self.

My father, who never touched alcohol, could not relate to any of this. No matter how much food he crammed down his gullet, he would never lose his family, his business, his ability to provide. My mother, who enjoyed a nightly cocktail or two, seemed to space out during these sessions. I, on the other hand, was a little sponge. I might as well have been an alcoholic, given the "identification" I felt with these tawdry stories, nodding my head in empathy and sympathy. To my young mind they seemed . . . authentic.

One week a kindly old alcoholic named Jimmy demonstrated his last-resort solution for stifling the urge to drink: "I just reach for my friend Mr. Snickers," he said, brandishing the chocolate bar. Not particularly helpful for us. Still, those old-timers helped explain the heart of the program, the twelve steps, which were posted on a laminated poster at the front of the room. In Step One, we admitted we were powerless over food and that our lives had become unmanageable. I loved that word: "unmanageable." I never would have characterized my life that way, but upon hearing this first commandment, I most certainly agreed.

The alcoholics also said that you couldn't really take Step One until you had hit bottom. If I had had the nerve to raise my hand and ask a question, I would have asked how you definitively know when you've hit bottom. I told myself that reaching 170 on the scale was hitting bottom, realizing that I weighed as much as my friend's father. But bottom for the alcoholics was always much more dramatic. One woman had had her children taken by social services. One guy told of losing his family business to gambling, his family to drink. I was only fifteen; the worst thing I had ever done was smoke pot and hoover a box of Yodels. *I am powerless over Hostess cakes and my life has become unmanageable.*

<hr />

I had been abstinent for five months when my parents and I attended an OA convention at Grossinger's, a Jewish resort in the Catskills. I was both embarrassed and proud to be a part of the proceedings. Among the teens in OA, I was considered somewhat of a poster child, having lost fifty pounds. I attended sessions on various topics, from "Working the Steps" and "What Is Higher Power?" to "HALT" (an acronym for "Hungry, Angry, Lonely, Tired") and "Nothing Tastes as Good as Abstinence Feels." But of all the new experiences and people I was exposed to that weekend, two women, for completely opposite reasons, made lasting impressions.

The first was the woman who emceed Talent Night. Short and extremely round, with dyed black hair gelled up in a punky style, she was a sarcastic, wisecracking precursor to Roseanne Barr or Rosie O'Donnell. Only she was the butt of her own jokes, and they were all about being fat. She fired off jokes like a machine gun in a nonstop barrage of self-inflicted wounds.

The other woman, a frail thin blond with wavy curls and slim arms, was a silent specter of a person. She kept her hands folded, as if in prayer. I wondered what her story was. She looked as if she had been thin her whole life. It wasn't until one of the last sessions of the weekend when she finally raised her hand to share. She stood slowly and in an almost inaudible voice said that she had been abstinent for three years and had lost nearly one hundred pounds. I couldn't believe it, seeing the slender, almost angelic woman before me. Then, she continued, she had slipped. That slip turned into six months of non-stop bingeing until she finally landed in a mental institution. She was here now, she said, because she has been abstinent for a year again, had lost the weight again, but lived in terror of falling off. She said all this without any affect to her voice, and I tried to conjure her a hundred pounds heavier, tried to imagine her inside the walls of an institution, tried to understand how this seemingly gentle, intelligent woman could have fallen from grace.

People jumped in to answer, reminding her to take it one day at a time. They told her to ask her Higher Power for help. I distanced myself from her and the whole discussion. I didn't want to know how a person could eat her way into a loony bin. I was interested in my own perfection. I wouldn't fall; I had this thing licked. At meetings I talked the humility talk and got lots of approval, but I felt nothing. No god, no gratitude. I was losing weight because I was working a perfect program and therefore was on my way to perfection. In those five months, I went from a size fourteen to a size six.

Then I packed my bags for a summer teen tour in Israel.

Most of the girls on the Israel trip were from Long Island. Their suitcases were filled with high heels, hot pants, and tons of makeup, in contrast to my shorts, jeans, army pants, and T-shirts. They had long nails and big hair. They were extremely flirtatious, especially with the stalwart Israeli soldiers. The ratio of girls to boys was twenty to four. Two of the boys were misfits and two were cute. One of the cute boys hooked up immediately with the ringleader of the girls, a kind of grown-up Jappy Pebbles with a red ponytail curled at the top of her head, a body-clinging leotard, and a gold chain dangling a Star of David at the crest of her enormous cleavage.

The other cute boy, Rick, took his time. Two weeks into the trip, he found me sitting alone under a tree, writing in my diary. He sat down.

"What are you writing?"

I shrugged in answer.

He pulled a pack of Marlboros out of his tight jeans and shook the pack in my direction.

"Thanks," I said, taking the dangling cigarette.

"Are you from the city?"

"Connecticut."

"Oh, fancy," he said.

"Where are you from?"

"Bronx." He held the fat blue flame of his Zippo

lighter up to my cigarette, then to his own. "The pizza here is a fuckin' joke."

I couldn't believe he was talking to me. Was lighting my cigarette. Rubbing his sneaker against mine. Rick had discovered a nearby Club Med and said I should meet him later that night—he could sneak us in. He tried to grab my diary, and I clutched it to my chest. He tried to pry it from my chest, and I rolled over on it. He straddled my back and tickled me. How could this be happening to me when I was standing over by the next tree watching myself?

That night we met as planned outside the Club Med. Rick had found a gash in the fence where we could slip in unnoticed, and he led me by the hand to it. Actually, he held my wrist as we walked the perimeter of the club; no boy had ever held my hand, and I was awkward and clumsy. *Take his hand,* I told myself, but I couldn't get my hand to move. Everything I thought to say failed to materialize into actual words. Many times that night he asked what I was thinking. I remained mute, and my silence acted as an aphrodisiac. Over the years I would talk too much on dates, nervous chatter pouring out like salt from the Dead Sea. But that first summer of love, I was everything a movie might have scripted: shy, aloof, enigmatic, a girl with a diary and a huge hunger for love wrapped up inside a silent stare.

food and loathing

It was July 14, Bastille Day, and the French-owned Club Med in the Israeli desert was celebrating with a lavish buffet of brie, grapes, lamb, and brioche. The sky burst with fireworks to commemorate the storming of those great prison walls. And in the midst of the celebration, a sixteen-year-old boy from the Bronx, a truant and pickpocket shipped off to Israel to get straightened out, lifted the face of a fifteen-year-old from suburban Connecticut, a girl who had already counted herself out in more ways than one, and pressed his sweet young lips to hers.

Rick stole pieces of lamb, hunks of cheese, and a bottle of wine, and we made off for the beach, where we ate and kissed and smoked, blowing long streams into the night sky. "I love this," he said, "right here between your hips and waist," and he ran his hand along the curve. I wanted to say, *I used to be fat,* but thought better of it. I wanted to tell him all about OA and how at Grossinger's a month earlier I had stood up in front of the whole twelve-step convention and been the teen star. I wanted to tell him how I had talked about my food compulsion in front of a packed auditorium and received a standing ovation. It seemed like a lifetime ago as I lay on that pebbly beach, staring at the stars.

I knew to keep it to myself. There was no pride in being a former fatty. If anything, it embarrassed me, and I was scared it would drive him away. I remained quiet, felt his body close to mine. I searched the starry night sky for a sign. For the first time I thought there must be a higher power. I didn't need any proof other than the cutest boy on the trip gazing into my eyes. Each night of the trip I was a little bolder, finally having all the experiences I had pretended to have during those torturous truth or dare games.

That summer I was the girl whom the other girls hated. One cornered me in a restroom and warned that I'd be lonely when he dumped me. I didn't care. I'd gladly take all the loneliness in the world for one slice of this cake.

As intoxicated as I was with Rick's attention, I also understood that we probably wouldn't see each other after we got home, that we lived too far apart. Too, I was fairly convinced that this summer was the product of an elaborate hoax. I had reinvented myself—my body, my demeanor, my way of being—for this short spell. At home, as the heavy girl, I was the mayor, friends with everyone, outspoken and funny. I had no idea how to let this new girl supplant her. As the summer drew to a close I was certain of only one thing: I wanted to return to my high school and temple woods girded with experience. I wanted to know what made the men and women in the movies I loved so full of passion. I wanted to bite from the tree of knowledge.

◇

After the summer, Rick and I visited each other once and then predictably drifted apart. When I got my period in September and knew for sure that I wasn't pregnant, I was both relieved and sad. The drama of my first love was over and the magical way I had felt leached from my body. Plus nothing seemed to have changed at home. Was it possible that no one realized I was a new person? I started making small exceptions in my eating regime and I was worried that doing so might lead to a greater fall.

Then, one afternoon, in the first weeks back at school, I ate something completely off the gray sheet guidelines. My friends and I had gotten high after school and were playing Frisbee on the soccer fields when a Good Humor truck pulled up, the saccharine bells chiming their little welcome song. I told myself I was only going to get a Tab, but suddenly I was devouring an ice cream sandwich: 120 calories.

It seemed innocent enough, just an ice cream sandwich to cure the munchies on a hot September afternoon, but what followed was nothing short of cataclysmic. I started bingeing that night with a force that was more intense than any previous overeating. I ate two bowls of Rice Krispies with tons of sugar, a bagel with peanut butter, half a box of Triscuits, and a stack of American cheese slices. Until that time I had definitely overeaten, no denying that. A five-foot-two girl doesn't blow up to 170 pounds without cramming a lot of food down her throat. But I had never made myself physically sick from overeating. I told myself to stuff it all in now because I had to start again on the program the very next day—Day One.

Suddenly I couldn't put together more than a week of abstinence. Then it was only a few days. I lied at the meetings, pretended I was on the program when I was slipping like crazy. When I got my driver's license, bingeing became even easier. I would sneak off to the Wawa Food Mart for all the junk food my mother never allowed in the house. I'd go to fast-food restaurants two towns away so as not to run into anyone. Peeling out of a Stop & Shop with a box of Yodels, I nearly mowed down an old lady. I ate until I was sick—often. And it became increasingly difficult to start over. My parents and I still attended meetings, but I was caught up in an elaborate ritual of procuring and eating forbidden foods. It became a highly clandestine and shame-filled act, including destroying the "evidence." I could never bring myself to fling my empty bags out of the car window onto the roadside. After bingeing in the privacy of my car, I'd search for a public garbage bin and furtively drop the contraband inside, like a criminal getting rid of evidence.

When I ate out at the local diner with friends, I never ordered what I really wanted. Everyone else would get a burger and fries while I ordered a salad. I knew this act of false self-denial was transparent. Having grown up overweight in a house that never had so much as a cookie on the kitchen shelves, I knew that the image of the fat girl eating salad was a sad paradox.

❧

I had eaten my way out of Paradise. Before too long I was unable to wear my size sixes, my eights, my tens. By winter I was back in my twelves and heading for the fourteens. I didn't know how to ask for help. I couldn't believe this was happening to me. Eventually, my moodiness and surliness compelled my parents to call Dr. Parker, a child psychiatrist at Yale.

It is true that I wanted to have real problems, wanted to be taken seriously. And I suspected that seeing a psychiatrist might make me deep. I often thought about suicide, but I had no idea if these thoughts were serious or what they meant.

One night, sitting on the hood of my car, I confided in my friend Benj. We passed a joint back and forth and watched the night sky become more vibrant.

"Do you ever think about it?" I asked.

"All the time."

"Me, too," I solemnly chimed in.

"I don't get people who *don't* think about it."

"Exactly," I said, and believed we were kindred spirits. Hansel and Gretel. Lisa and David.

"Did you ever think about actually doing it?"

"Yeah."

"What stops you?"

"I don't know. My parents, I guess."

"How would you do it?"

"Maybe hang myself."

"Oh, god," I said, and shuddered to imagine my handsome friend dangling from a rope like Perry in *In Cold Blood,* his head bent over, his pants soiled.

For all my thoughts of killing myself, I had never formulated a plan. I told Benj that my parents were sending me to a shrink, and he burst out laughing.

"They're so fucked up."

I laughed, too, coughing on the drag I had just inhaled. I was in love with Benj, but I knew he was sleeping with every girl in our school. Still, I loved being around him; I envied his wild, rebellious spirit. If the rest of us took two tabs of acid, he took twelve. If we stayed out partying until one in the morning, he'd discover some after-hours club and stay out all night. He seemed to have a whole secret life away from our Frisbee fields and basement lairs. He had an electric energy, and watching him play air guitar to the Doors made me briefly envision him as the young Jim Morrison, his smooth hairless chest pulsating with the music: *You know that you can get much higher.* And when he'd sneak over in the middle of a school night and tap on the window of my basement bedroom, I'd follow him to one of our secret spots to get high and have one of our long philosophical talks.

Dr. Parker had an owly face and a stunning collection of paisley and plaid socks. He wore a floppy bow tie, also paisley, and usually, while I talked, he'd hold one hand in the other and admire his beautifully pared nails. I saw that I got his full attention only when I talked about sex, a subject on which I was now an expert.

Once I told him about two boys, best friends, whom

I had had an enormous crush on in junior high. Jonas, a dreamy, gentle boy, was one of the smartest kids in our school. David was more flamboyant, an attention-getter. Their easy bond was enviable.

"Which one would you have liked to go out with?" Dr. Parker asked.

I thought for a while. They were both cute, and both intrigued me for different reasons. I also knew that my chances of dating either one was nil.

"Whichever one liked me," I finally answered.

"But which would *you* like?"

Didn't he realize I had no choice in the matter? Girls like me didn't choose. *How could he be so stupid?* We spent the rest of the session in our usual silence.

That evening after therapy, I found myself at McDonald's. They had just installed a drive-through window, which was nothing short of a miracle to me. As a small child had I not fantasized about such Jetson-like inventions? It was a dream come true to get fries without leaving the car, to talk into an anonymous box and have a cheeseburger handed through a window. I no longer ran the risk of running into someone from math class inside, or worse, some Mrs. Mankowicz type who would run her evil eye over my figure as she calculated the caloric quantity of my order.

food and loathing

Waiting for my order of large fries and a chocolate shake, I thought about Dr. Parker's question about which boy I liked more. I was ashamed of my answer: *Whichever one liked me.* The more I thought about my response, the more despondent I became. Fortunately, the first bite of McDonald's was like heroin, the salt and grease combining in a hot explosion that traveled right to the pain center and wiped it out. All feeling was numbed as the potato sticks, like tiny soldiers, decimated the emotional terrain, leaving me bloated, drugged, transported. After finishing the last fry, I'd reach into the empty bag in search of any cold strays and eat them, too. Only now the thrill was gone. Recrimination was setting in even as I premeditated my next bite. *Which one would I choose? Who was he kidding?*

That night, after my parents went to bed, I made one of my concoctions, deploying all manner of forbidden food. I slathered a piece of bread with peanut butter, then drizzled it with frozen chocolate chips that my mother kept for baking, and toasted it until the chocolate made a shiny puddle on top—my version of a Reese's bar. Other times I'd cook up a whole pot of noodles and eat it with butter and cheese. One time, hearing my parents wake up, I ran with the pot into the garage, leaving the noodles under the car until the coast was clear.

My Lonely Country

I was in charge of a fundraiser for B'nai B'rith Girls. We were selling chocolate bars, thick blocks wrapped in gold foil. I kept my supply in my car trunk to keep from eating them—a good but short-lived plan. One night, after just a few days with the contraband in my trunk, I threw my mother's mink over my pajamas and tiptoed into the frozen night to retrieve a bar. Just one bar at first, eventually three and four. I raised a small fortune for the cause.

✦

Dr. Parker made the diagnosis of manic depression. I didn't know what to do with the information. Wasn't I a poseur? Wasn't my behavior just a teenager's bid for attention? Wouldn't I be happy if I could just get thin again? I thought only grownups could be manic-depressive. Yes, I wanted to be taken seriously, but this diagnosis and the medication he prescribed scared me. I knew I hated myself, but I also didn't want to swallow anything that would change me. Some small part of me knew that the real Betsy existed inside this overweight miserable girl. And I was afraid that the lithium would change or destroy me, the way drugs nearly destroyed Jack Nicholson in *One Flew Over the Cuckoo's Nest*.

I thought of the sorrowful woman at the OA convention who had described her out-of-control eating and eventual breakdown. *That's not me,* I told myself. *That's just not me. If I could just put together a few weeks of abstinence, get back that pure feeling, that's all I need.* Instead, I was sitting in a psychiatrist's office, unable to speak. I thought of the girl I had been just a few months earlier, standing under the blue Israeli sky in her one-piece bathing suit while everyone pranced around in bikinis. She hadn't even really known who she was or might yet be. I thought of her in that small cot giving up her virginity, trying to shed everything and become someone else. In such a small space of time I had gone from one extreme to another, and now I was headed back to a place I knew too well: my lonely country.

Scared out of their minds at the doctor's diagnosis, my parents signed a consent form and the pills were prescribed. My heart would be tested first to monitor the effect of the medication. I didn't understand what the medication would do to my brain, how it could change me or help me. Dr. Parker never fully explained manic depression to me. Instead, he warned me that if I didn't take lithium I would wind up in a mental hospital by the time I was in my twenties. I don't know if that warning set me on the course that followed. But I've always believed that his off-hand remark, made with absolute certainty and no sensitivity to its power over an impressionable teenager, was the dramatic equivalent of introducing a gun into the first act of my young life.

Three

The Watery Floor

The examination room was the standard mix of white walls, white linoleum floors, and stainless steel. Only a thin stretch of white paper lay between my body and the stainless steel table. My naked back and buttocks stuck to the paper. I imagined myself a piece of meat at the butcher's, ready to be weighed and wrapped up. I imagined myself a cadaver, a drowned girl fished out of the river, my body bloated, small twigs stuck in my long, tangled hair, my lips purple-black. I imagined myself playing Frisbee on a wide green field with my friends, stoned and completely free for those few moments when my wrist snapped and the Frisbee sailed from my hand into the air in a perfect arc.

My friends didn't know that I had been seeing a shrink. They thought I was busy with my many extracurricular lessons: pottery, drama, piano. They didn't know that at home I had become "uncommunicative," or had they really registered that after losing fifty pounds, I'd put it all back on and more. After all, I was thin for such a brief time, just the summer I spent in Israel, far away from my little gang. And now, in the months since I'd returned, I was pulling out the old jeans, the old uniform. I hid my body beneath my baggy clothes while I gained all the weight back, like a teenager trying to hide her pregnancy. Only I wasn't pregnant.

My look was quasi–Janis Joplin, my hair wild around my face, my wire-rimmed glasses tinted brown. I always had a joint to smoke and I was better at Frisbee than most of the boys. I had a 1976 brown Monte Carlo with a bong in the glove compartment. My life with my friends revolved around getting stoned, listening to the Grateful Dead, and playing Frisbee. Only we weren't a pack of troubled kids like the ones in *River's Edge* or *The Outsiders*. We were from solid New Haven families (none of our parents had yet divorced), we generally got good grades, and we expected to attend college. Though we had different levels of ability and ambition, we were in no way lost. Rather, we were all fairly spoiled, privileged kids with too much time and access to Acapulco Gold. We had no interest in law or business, but we weren't joining the Peace Corps either. We were sexually promiscuous, and by twelfth grade most of us had lost our virginity and taken acid more than a few times.

As I lay on the table, I wondered about my friends. What would they think if they knew that a young medical technician was squirting clear gel on plastic pads and pressing them to my body? Did they have any idea how I dreamed of leaving them behind on the playing fields of our high school and never coming back?

When another technician mistakenly barged in, I pulled the paper gown over my exposed breast. Words of apology were mumbled and the technician readjusted a suction cup. Everything about this scene was wrong. The lights above me started to spin and dance like the shards inside a kaleidoscope finding a new pattern. I wanted the technician to stop, break his rhythm, but he seemed to be picking up speed. I momentarily flashed on him as Gene Wilder in *Young Frankenstein,* and when a nurse came in I imagined her as Madeline Kahn with a streaked beehive hairdo and jet-black, juicy lips. In my fantasy they were

madly dancing around my body, squirting clear gel everywhere as the pin on the EKG machine started to fluctuate
wildly. The fantasy ended with a shock of electricity
going through me, my eyelids fluttering as my body
bolted upright. When I tried to speak, blood spilled out.

"Are you okay there?" the young man asked me.

I barely nodded in assent. Was I okay? I wasn't sure
how my life had come to this. I wanted it to be other, but
I didn't know what "other" was. Just a few months ago I
was making out with my first boyfriend and now I was
this bloated, corpse-like thing being prepped for an EKG,
a prerequisite for the medication my shrink wanted me
to take.

Only I hadn't planned on disrobing in an examination room, hadn't planned on Dr. Parker telling my parents everything I said or inviting them in when he told
me I had to take lithium. I hadn't planned on my parents
signing waivers to facilitate all this.

I watched the young man continue his work while
avoiding all eye contact with me. His lab coat sported a
pocket protector for pens, and he wore crepe-soled
shoes, two crimes our high school tribunal would have
hanged him for. Still, I wanted him to save me. And in
the silence between us, the room nearly exploded with
the sound of his footsteps methodically squinging their

way around the table, the gurgling of the gel as he squeezed it out of the tube, the tiny sucking air pops as he placed the suction cups on my bare chest. I was relieved that my nipples were pert. Thank god the room was freezing. The last thing I needed would have been for my boobs to sag while he worked. Why did my life suck so much?

He asked again if I was okay, and a tear fell out of the corner of my eye. He didn't see it or brush it away, nor did he gently cradle my head and smooth my hair. He didn't lift me and cover me with my medical gown and carry me out of there like Dustin Hoffman at the end of *The Graduate* or Richard Gere at the end of *An Officer and a Gentleman*. He was just this guy in a white coat doing his job, hooking me up to an EKG machine for a procedure I would have to repeat every three months to monitor the effect of the medication on my heart.

He switched on the machine, and the metal arm danced across a strip of paper. Imagining that the contraption was a lie detector test, I interrogated myself with questions, watching the machine respond in inky peaks and valleys: Did I belong here? Was I a faker? Was I after attention? Did I do this to myself? Was I to blame? Was I crazy?

food and loathing

What exactly was a nervous breakdown anyway? I had
read Fitzgerald's *The Crack-Up* and was in love with Ann
Sexton's poems. How many times had I read *The Bell Jar*,
always feeling a little disappointed when Esther Green-
wood finally asserts her lust for life: "I took a deep breath
and listened to the old brag of my heart. I am I am I am."
So what if my heart beat out the opposite pulse, the bratty
retort *I'm not I'm not I'm not.* The influence of the confessional poets was undeniable, and by the tenth grade I fan-
cied myself a young poet. That said, I couldn't imagine
actually winding up in a hospital. In spite of my fascina-
tion with the darker impulses, I saw myself as someone
who was strong.

People had commented on my so-called strength
my whole life. When I was a little girl, my mother would
describe me as willful. "Bathing you," she would say,
"was like wrestling an alligator." And I would conjure this
image of myself, half-girl, half-reptile, thrashing about in
the bathtub, my eyes slits.

At sleep-away camp, a counselor whom I adored for
her wild streak, silver bangles, and peasant blouses would
wake me up when she got back from a date. We'd sit on
the big rock behind the bunk and she'd let me smoke her

Newports as she told me all about her date, how she almost went all the way.

"Why am I telling you this?" Marti would say, lighting one cigarette off another.

I smiled, probably a little uncertain myself, but thrilled to be taken into her confidence.

"I don't even know if I love him."

"You love him," I said. "He's the coolest guy here." Everyone was in love with Ray, and I was proud that my counselor had attracted him. Ray was a tall, thin college senior with blue eyes and a gentle touch. He was almost shy. He didn't have to do anything to win the easy love of his own bunk or the adoration of most of the girls at camp.

Marti beamed. "You're right. I just don't know what's going to happen after camp."

"You'll stay together."

"You think?"

I nodded my head strenuously, though I had no idea what would happen.

"How did you get to be so wise?" she asked.

Inwardly I thought, *Yes, she has recognized my true self.* But of course the smaller voice was there, too. *I'm not so wise. Surely you can see that I'm just a little girl.*

The medication made me feel slow. The corridors of my high school were out of focus, the walls turned spongy and breathed. I wasn't sure if my reaction was real or imagined. They could have given me a placebo; I was that suggestible. I complained to Dr. Parker about the side effects and he said to give it time, my brain needed to adjust. I was terrified the lithium was going to change my essential self, though at the same time I was desperate to change.

One night I confided in Benj about the medication, to see how this news would play on my friend and confidant. We were in my car because the night had turned cold. The dashboard glowed faintly, WPLR playing "Stairway to Heaven."

"My shrink wants me to try medication," I started.

"Can I get some?"

"It's not that kind of medication. You don't get high."

"Why bother?"

I punched Benj and we both laughed. Lit cigarettes.

"I guess help with my depression."

"You're not depressed," he said, leaning over to kiss my forehead. "You're one of the best people in the whole world."

With that, Benj took a tiny brick of tinfoil from his jacket and unwrapped it to reveal what looked like a miniature chunk of peat moss. He told me it was opiated hash he had gotten in the city. After smoking it we had sex for the first—and only—time.

The next morning, alone in bed with the smell of Benj and the hash mingling on my skin, my mouth a dry furnace, I knew I had made a big mistake. Having sex wouldn't change anything between us. I knew my weight kept me from being girlfriend material. The only thing that would make things better was abstinence. I had to get back on my program. Losing weight wasn't just about getting thin, it was about achieving perfection. Which meant two things and two things alone: my mother's love and the attention of boys. Was there anything else in life to want?

So with all the teenage self-righteousness at my command, I convinced myself that my shrink was an idiot who didn't have the first clue about me, and I flushed my medication down the toilet.

Everyone has a fighting weight, a range she considers acceptable, if not ideal. For me this was 140 to 155 pounds. I managed to graduate from high school and arrive at New York University at my fighting weight. More miraculously, I managed to stay within my fighting range all through my four years there. I managed this by

going back and forth between bingeing and total abstinence. Four days on, three days off. Three weeks on, one
week off. I was always gaining and losing the same fifteen
pounds within the range. There was much I could
accomplish in that range. I could fit into the size tens and
twelves in my wardrobe, which doubtless resembled the
closets of many women who struggle with their weight:
filled with increasingly stylish clothes in the smaller sizes
and more muumuu-like cover-ups at the high end. I had
a collection of black jeans, skirts, sweaters, and tops in
sizes from six to fourteen, a collection of pantyhose that
ranged from small to queen to control-top girdle, the
kind that leaves you dizzy and gasping for air when you
finally roll them off at the end of the day.

I found that when my weight was within the range I
could be of the world. I could go to my English classes
and take notes, could concentrate enough to read and
write papers. While I couldn't overtly flirt at my fighting
weight, I could interest certain kinds of men. Mostly lon-
ers and artists, bookish guys. I never had a relationship
that lasted more than a few weeks or months, but I had a
number of liaisons. I never felt particularly good about
myself—that would have been pushing it—but I could
function. I passed.

The Watery Floor

I lived in a dorm with a roommate who spent all her time listening to Deep Purple or The Boss. My best friend down the hall shared my love of barbiturates and supplied us with a steady stream of Percodan from her physician father. I went to poetry readings. I joined a writing group with three fellow students who met in a tiny West Village apartment that had a loft bed and a pink refrigerator. I haunted the Strand, a used-book store, where I would lose myself in its endless, dusty stacks, and drink cappuccinos for hours at Café Dante while writing in my journal.

Yet no matter where I was, whether sitting in class or in the cafeteria at the student center, I wondered if my food addiction was ultra-obvious. I wondered if anyone could tell from looking at me that I had binged all weekend, that every waking moment when I wasn't bingeing was spent in the service of staying abstinent, getting back on the program. I led a double life—attending classes, going to the library, getting high and sleeping with guys, then slipping off to church basements for OA meetings, where I joined the great anonymous overweight.

I studied the faces of fellow students, trying to piece together how anyone was able to live free of obsession. I wondered who among us felt normal, who else was in therapy. Whose mother loved him? Who had a pencil dick? Would any of my classmates at NYU suspect that I was running to an OA meeting after classes one day, cramming cookies down my throat the next? Sometimes I ate so fast I had to remind myself to slow down. I'd tell myself, you don't want to pull a Mama Cass—anything but that. It didn't matter that Cass had died of a heroin overdose; she would always be remembered for choking on a ham sandwich because she was fat.

Yet to all appearances, I functioned, even excelled. No one would have suspected that I read *Anna Karenina* twice in a row because I found the ending more beautiful than tragic. That I saw *'night, Mother* four times on Broadway and never cried, knowing that the character played by Kathy Bates was better off killing herself. That although I was no longer taking medication, I had begun to see a new shrink. My mother had found Dr. Mizner for me. She was worried about the abrupt end of my visits with Dr. Parker, and when my depressive phases returned she grew grave. I didn't really know what I would get out of seeing Dr. Mizner, since I believed that abstinence, and abstinence alone, would set me free.

I had a minor breakthrough in my junior year, when our writing professor assigned us to write a sestina, that highly unpopular verse form using six-line stanzas in which the end words of the stanza are repeated in varied order. I wrote a poem titled "Calories and Other Counts," in which I described my food obsession, albeit in a lighthearted way with a feminist gloss. Until then my weight problem was the last thing I would have revealed about myself. I even read the poem in a poetry slam at a popular downtown venue. I pushed myself to take the stage in the open-mike session and chanted out my poem, my personal "Howl." Surely this was progress.

When I took my seat, a cute guy two seats over stretched his arm around me and whispered, "Baby, you're not fat." I wish I could tell you that he and I made our way to his East Village apartment and made passionate love all night. Instead, I looked at him as if he had a third eye and fled the club for a nearby bodega, where I picked up a package of my best friend, Little Debbie brownies.

Long weekends were my downfall. On Labor Day before senior year, I ate my way through an eightplex, going from movie to movie with a new box of Milk Duds or Junior Mints or a bucket of popcorn for every show. And on the single Thanksgiving of my life that I didn't spend with my family (my OA group had endorsed the choice—families are generally considered highly toxic to "recovering" types), instead of going to extra meetings and taking care of myself, I started the holiday by having two full breakfasts—buttered bagel, scrambled eggs, fries, and bacon—at two different diners in the Village.

That particular lost day ended with a midnight visit to a deli on First Avenue, wearing only my raincoat. In my rush to get more food I forgot to wear my glasses—something I had never done before. I didn't realize my mistake until I reached the street and found the world an unfocused, bleeding mess. I clutched at my coat—did I really leave the apartment with nothing on underneath? I knew I should go back for my glasses or, better yet, go home and stay there. I had been eating nonstop all day. But in the window of thought when I might have considered that sober course, the compulsion was urging me on down the street. *Just one more thing. Day One starts tomorrow.* Only I wasn't interested in tomorrow. I wanted only to wipe out the present. Or to go back to the time when Rick was running his finger along my protruding hipbone. Where was Rick now? Where was my hipbone?

I wanted to slip inside the deli unseen, gather my items, and disappear. I spent a great deal of time cruising delis, looking for a counterman who wouldn't make a sarcastic remark about my purchases: *Hungry? Nice little appetite you've got there.* How had I come to care more about the deli man's opinion than about how I looked to the hundreds of men I passed in the street as I ate my way through Manhattan? Now, however, I didn't just want to disappear temporarily, I wanted to turn up in the Hudson. A girl with no identification, found floating in her trench coat— another sad news item in the *New York Post*.

I grabbed two thick Hershey bars and asked for three croissants. The counterman smirked. I threw a twenty on the counter and fled. I heard him calling after me about my change, but I ran across the street oblivious to the oncoming traffic, a blur of lights and horns with me in the headlights, my bag of food already grease-stained from the croissants, wishing those cars would plow me under and end the daily battle. And through the confusion, the lights, and the blare, I heard those compassionate New York voices: *Get the fuck out of the way! What's your fucking problem?*

⁂

The haircut set me off. Somewhere during spring break of my senior year I walked into St. Mark's 24-Hour Hair Salon after seeing the midnight show of *Shoot the Moon*, one of the rare movies that dared to portray children as the beasts they are. Albert Finney and Diane Keaton actually seemed married, so palpable was their mutual hostility. I had been spending all my nights that winter of 1982 at the library, where I alternately read, wrote terrible poems, smoked, and husked sunflower seeds while pretending to concentrate on my studies. The library was my refuge from an imploded social life. In four years I hadn't so much made friends as gone through them. I was staying away from the apartment because my roommate had finally found a lover, and the two of them spent endless hours in bed, the sounds of their lovemaking reverberating through our doorless railroad flat.

Every night after the library closed, I'd see whatever was playing at the St. Mark's midnight show. Then home, hopefully late enough to avoid the coital chorus. I figured I would ride out that depression as I had so many times before. That night, though, I made the instantly regretted decision to sit down in a barber chair and let a guy with badly capped teeth and a diamond pinkie ring transform my shoulder-length wavy brown hair into cole slaw, chopping away as if my head were an actual cabbage. My worldview certainly encompassed the idea that I deserved whatever I got, that whatever malaise I suffered I had brought on myself, but no one deserved a haircut like the one the butcher of lower Broadway gave me that night.

I spent my final semester traipsing from class to class with my hair hidden under my sweatshirt hood. The prospect of graduating seemed like a cruel joke; how could I graduate when I was only nominally there? Could I have gone through four years of college without giving a second thought to what I would do when I finished? My parents told me I would have to get a job if I wanted to stay in the city. They'd pay my rent for the summer, but that was it. That semester I made a number of lame attempts to look for work, even swallowing my pride and setting up an appointment with the daughter of one of my mother's friends, an editor in a large publishing house.

I rode my bike to the interview and was locking it out front when my eye caught a Häagen-Dazs sign across the street. I glanced at my watch and bolted for the ice-cream store. As I waited in reception, I noticed that the chocolate cone I had gobbled down in record time had stained my plaid dress—vaguely camouflaged, thank god, by the busy pattern. I made a mental note for future interviews: vanilla.

With a brisk step and too-tight smile, Ronnie came out to meet me in reception. I could tell immediately that she was seeing me just to be polite, as a favor to her mother. I marveled at how put-together she was, wearing a crisp pantsuit and creamy blouse, with three inches of gold bangle bracelets that jangled like a rainstick as she lifted her arms to hang my rain slicker on the back of her office door. She held the slicker out as if it were a dirty diaper, and I instantly realized how ludicrous it was to wear the slicker anywhere but summer camp.

My whole life could be charted in accessory crimes and misdemeanors. It's a miracle I was never singled out in the *Glamour* "Don't" column, that monthly feature in which a few girls were pictured for some fashion gaffe, like wearing the wrong-colored hose or carrying too large a handbag. The photos were taken of real women by some roving photographer who snapped his victims usually crossing a busy street, and the snapshots of the offenders appeared in the magazine with their faces obscured by a black strip. I always thought my mother could have invented this column. She loved nothing more than to identify the one marring element in an otherwise perfectly coordinated outfit. Just as the magazine pointed out a girl wearing the wrong shoes, my mother was quick to notice fashion transgressions.

Looking at Ronnie, I knew she was exactly what my mother would have ordered up in a daughter. A girl who had a pair of pumps in every color and a bag to match. A girl who could position a brooch and drape a scarf. Her hair was Farrah Fawcett perfect, and when her phone rang she picked it up and confidently said, "Ronnie Samuels." To this day I have never been able to answer my phone that way: *Betsy Lerner.* In part, it seems idiotic. What am I, Macy's? But then it seemed way too grown up.

It hadn't even occurred to me to prepare for the interview, only now I could see that Ronnie was working hard to compensate for my lack of questions, my lack of everything. When she asked what kind of books interested me, I sat in a frozen panic. I couldn't name a book to save my life. Fiction or nonfiction, she prodded me further. All I could think of was poetry, but I figured out not to say so, amid the foil and embossed jackets that decorated her shelves.

"Do you like women's fiction?" she asked.

Looking still more pained, I said, "What do you mean?"

She rattled off names of trashy writers I'd never go near. "You know, Danielle Steele, Jackie Collins, Judith Krantz."

"I like Philip Roth," I said, my voice full of hope.

I left her office with a bunch of thrillers and a good deal of advice about résumé writing and typing skills. I dumped the books in a trash can on the corner. Then, panicked that she would see them on her way home, I retrieved them, only to toss them in another can a few blocks east.

Ronnie had made it clear that typing was the ticket, but I was a lousy typist. I stopped at a stationer and bought a box of cream-colored paper and envelopes. I even signed up for a typing class in Brooklyn. I spent the better part of April typing letters and résumés on my two-tone Smith-Corona and sending them to the human resources departments at major publishing houses. I made tons of errors, and the Wite-Out I gobbed on to hide the mistakes looked like Clearasil painted on a pimple. I didn't know about cream-colored Wite-Out. I didn't know I could take my letters to a typing service. I wouldn't allow myself to toss that stupid cream paper and exchange it for white. After all, it was expensive. Instead, I spent night after night typing letters, throwing away ten for every one I got right. It was slow, painstaking work, which ultimately yielded exactly three interviews—at all of which I failed the typing test.

Then there was Milton. I was in an advanced seminar on the seventeenth-century poet, and right up until the end I was doing fine. I was in love with the shorter poems and with "Lycidas," parts of which I memorized and would chant to myself as I walked through the Village from class to the library and home:

> *Weep no more, woeful shepherds, weep no more,*
> *For Lycidas, your sorrow, is not dead,*
> *Sunk though he be beneath the watery floor;*
> *So sinks the day-star in the ocean bed.*

It was the final paper, on the narrator in *Paradise Lost,* that stopped me. I should have been able to crank out the paper in a week. But something happened when I began the first sentence: *The narrator in Milton's Paradise Lost serves to.* Again. *The narrator in Milton's Paradise Lost works as. The narrator in Milton's Paradise Lost functions as.* I filled three legal pads this way, each fresh attempt bringing on greater anxiety. I'd step outside the library to smoke. I'd get more candy from the vending machines, cruising the refreshment area until I was certain no one I knew was around. I'd surreptitiously pop m&m's in my mouth and begin again: *Milton's narrator . . . Milton's narrator . . .* By the end of the month the pad on my middle finger where I pressed my pen was flat and shiny. My legal pads were quilted with writing. My hair was a freak show, part Medusa, part Art Garfunkle.

Making matters worse, the three other members of

my West Village writing group were headed for great things: Alice, our leader and self-styled Gertrude Stein, was off to the Cape to write screenplays; Sandy, the play-wright, had a full-time job lined up at Grove Press, home of Beckett and Miller and other writers I worshiped; John, whom I knew the least, had a full fellowship to NYU's graduate school in the English department.

I decided, in desperation, to apply to graduate schools, so I made an appointment with the head of NYU's literature division. The dean looked at me in dis-belief. "Applications were filled out in the fall."

Not knowing what to say, I stared at the brass inkwell on his desk, on which rested a Montblanc pen as fat as a cigar.

"Let's suppose this were the fall, just for fun, what area of study would you be interested in, Miss Lerner?"

It was the publishing interview all over again. I went blank. Fortunately, the dean was interrupted with a phone call. As I looked at the high windows of his office, they turned from clear to clouded in a split second, the office darkening to a soupy green with the changing light.

"Sorry about that," he said, returning the earpiece to the cradle. "So, Miss Lerner, what is it you think you might take up?"

Miraculously I summoned an answer and ventured that I liked poetry.

"What period?" he asked.

"Modern," I said, thinking that I was getting the hang of this.

He asked which poets. *Plath, Sexton, and Lowell,* I was thinking, but I would not name them. Any affinity to these confessional poets would stereotype me as a certain kind of moody female, and I wanted to avoid that association at all costs. Instead I produced the names of a few modern poets who were then popular among students. "Philip Levine, Gerald Stern, Galway Kinnell."

The dean removed his bifocals with an expression of pained disbelief and dropped them on the desk as if they were of no use to him. Then he leaned across the desk and sneered, "Contemporary, Miss Lerner, those are contemporary poets."

Fuck.

The first weekend in May I went home, mostly to take a physical break from everything that was oppressing me at school—my roommate situation, the city, the failed typing efforts. I stayed in my childhood bedroom, trying to write the Milton paper, trying not to let on that all I wanted was to squirrel away with a blanket and pillows and barricade myself in the crawlspace beneath the stairs, where I had spent many long hours hiding as a child. I could tell my parents were worried about me, but everyone, including myself, believed I would pull through. When my father knocked and came into my room, I started crying. I told him about the paper and how afraid I was that I wouldn't graduate.

My father picked up the copy of *Paradise Lost* and started reading it. Neither a college graduate nor a big reader, he must have experienced those lines of poetry as utterly incomprehensible. But he persisted, his eyes moving down the page until he finally stopped and looked at me.

"Honey, what is it you're supposed to write?"

I told him that the narrator is a literary device and I was supposed to show how Milton used this device to different effect throughout the poem.

"You can do that, can't you, honey?"

"I don't know, Daddy."

He lifted the book again and tried to read a few more lines. I couldn't bear watching my father puzzle over the text. He had worked every day of his life since he was a teenager, first driving a lumber truck, eventually running and owning lumber yards of his own. In our family his success was near-mythic. My mother often described his negotiating abilities as Solomon-like, and there was nothing he couldn't do or provide for his family. But I knew he couldn't do this. I knew those lines of text were beyond him, and I started crying again as I watched my father try to help me, his brow furrowed in concentration as he held the worn pink paperback in his freckled hand.

Then he pushed my hair out of my face and looked at me. I'm not sure what he saw just then: his little girl filled with hope or his hopeless little girl. I knew he would have done anything humanly possible to help me. I wanted so badly to be his little girl again, quizzing him from Playbills about the casts of the Broadway shows we had seen, getting up with him before seven, the early risers of the family, and watching him crack an egg one-handed, fry it up with salami for me.

He wiped my tears and asked me to try for him. I said I would. When he left the room, I crawled under the blankets and watched the sky darken. Headlights from cars passing along the road circled the room like searchlights. When I was nine and ten years old I would pretend I was Anne Frank and the car lights were the Nazis' flashlights searching the house for Jews. I'd lie perfectly still, my heart knocking in my chest as I imagined the snatches of German conversation ricocheting in the rooms and hall below, the sound of boots mounting the stairs.

My mother woke me in time to get the train back to the city. On the car ride to the station, she told me that she had called Dr. Mizner. I was outraged that she would call my psychiatrist behind my back, and I learned that it wasn't the first time. Dr. Mizner had told her not to worry, I was going through a very typical case of seniori-tis. It happens to the best of them, he told her. He said I was absolutely fine. I wasn't so certain. And something told me that if I filled one more page with aborted attempts to define Milton's narrator, I was going to off myself.

Some weeks later I heard the news. The valedicto-rian of my high school class, a brilliant boy on his way to medical school, had gassed himself in his parents' garage. Not only had he graduated first in our class, he was at the top of his class at an Ivy League college. I wasn't friends with him, though we had gone to Hebrew school together for years, but I knew he was one of the truly brilliant among us. I always believed that my own suc-cesses were as dependent on my sense of humor and abil-ity to please as on any native ability. Even finishing the

The Watery Floor

Milton paper and graduating seemed more a feat of will than anything else. I went to the bathroom in my apartment and stared at myself in the streaked mirror above the sink. I kept looking at myself, hoping to see a face I would recognize. I thought about my classmate and wondered what combination of pressure and depression had led to his final act, how a boy that brilliant could not find worth in his own life. I knew then that the sea was more vast and watery than Milton knew to tell.

Four

Crying Wolf

Entering the mausoleum-like lobby of Dr. Mizner's building, with its somber lighting, made me feel highly suspicious. I wasn't old enough or rich enough to be here; my problems couldn't have been worth $120 an hour. Then there was Bob. Bob the Doorman. When I first started seeing Mizner, I understood that his doorman had to stop me and direct me to Mizner's suite. But after a few months of regular visits, it irritated me beyond reason that he refused to recognize me. The drill should have been unexceptional: I would nod at Bob upon arrival, the smile clamped on my face acknowledging that just as surely as I recognized him, he must certainly recognize me. All I wanted was to be let in without further ado. But no. Each week Bob would physically block my path, popping out from his lectern-style reception desk like a jack-in-the-box, and ask me who I had come to see.

"Dr. Mizner," I'd say as softly as possible, especially if any tenants were hovering.

"Mizner," Bob would repeat, sounding to my self-conscious ears as if he were announcing it through a bull-horn. Even more annoying was his little charade of looking up Dr. Mizner's name in his directory and telling me what floor to go to.

"It's okay," I'd say. "I know where to go."

"Lemme just check for you, miss. Just a second, miss," he'd say, lifting one hand in a stop sign to make sure I got the message.

I'd wait, surveying the Brillo pad of hair that was molded across his scalp and his massive aviator glasses, joined at the bridge with a swath of filthy, ancient masking tape.

After a few months I could barely make eye contact with Bob or mumble a thank-you after he directed me inside. Instead I kept my eyes on the rugs that led to Dr.

Crying Wolf

Mizner's elevator bank. While waiting for the elevator, various fantasies would play out, all of which involved my inflicting bodily harm on Bob. Sometimes I'd rip the glasses from his craggy face and twist them in half, shove that filthy piece of masking tape up one of his nostrils. Or roll him up in one of the long, beautiful carpets and set it aflame.

I took some comfort from Dr. Mizner's waiting room, which was furnished with low couches and one enormous wooden coffee table piled with thick magazines like *Architectural Digest* and *Smithsonian*. The room was always empty, but the goings-on behind his office wall never failed to hold my attention. The woman who had the session before mine often sobbed loudly, and though I was desperate to know her anguish, I didn't dare move to the couch next to the wall, where I'd be closer to the sound. Her crying was very moving, and I imagined her as a handsome blonde with whom Mizner was in love. Sometimes I imagined her as Meryl Streep in *Sophie's Choice,* with her delicious Polish accent and malleable face. Sometimes I'd picture her as Gena Rowlands in one of Cassavetes's films, hard and beautiful, with that square jaw, capable of great sorrow and meanness. In the absence of knowing what a person looked like, I invested him or her with great beauty and power.

Though Mizner wasn't particulary good-looking, his features worked together to make him seem much greater than the sum of his individual parts. For starters, he was tall, and height had always been a big attraction for me. My mother often said short girls like me should leave the tall guys to the tall girls. But I wanted a tall man, a man who was bigger than me, physically imposing. I liked feeling small, enveloped. Mizner was tall and a little beefy. He kept his salt-and-pepper hair long and scraggly in a quasi-shag, and his beard so closely cropped that it looked soft like moss, and I often wanted to touch it. His wardrobe consisted mostly of gray slacks and sport jackets, knit ties, argyle socks and, of all things, beige saddle shoes. But it worked for him.

His office was simply decorated, his furniture all clean lines and ninety-degree angles. He parked himself in a black leather Eames chair, which tilted back dangerously. A small tear at the seam along the seat exposed the white stuffing within, like a man's boxer shorts caught in his fly. Everything else in the office was neat and beautiful. The piles of journals on his desk were perfectly stacked. His bookcase was filled but not stuffed. The deep red Oriental carpets warmed the oak floor.

In our early sessions I generally focused on my weight and my inability to stay abstinent. Dr. Mizner took the view that everyone could stand to lose some weight, himself included.

"But it's not just about food," I'd try to explain. Abstinence had become a moral issue, a survival issue. "My whole life revolves around bingeing and staying abstinent. I don't know how to live anymore."

"Betsy," Dr. Mizner would say, "food is fuel. It's simple."

I'd try to explain about OA, the twelve steps.

"If OA is helpful, fine, but it's just a diet."

He didn't understand. I just sat there. Where was this going?

"You don't understand. I feel like I'm going to die when I'm not on the program," I said, my voice going high and weak, nearly pleading for him to understand the urgency I felt as each day degenerated into another binge, another raft of self-loathing delivered to my shores.

"I just don't think it would be helpful for me to buy into your sense of urgency," he said. "I could lose a few pounds, too. I don't know why you let it bother you so much?"

"I can't be happy when I'm overweight. It's that simple."

"Why not?"

"Because. I just can't."

"A person can be happy at any weight."

"Maybe you can."

"No, Betsy, weight does not have to impact on personal happiness."

"You're just wrong. There are no truly happy fat people. There aren't. They may act happy, but it's a lie."

"What about Pavarotti?"

"Fuck Pavarotti."

&

Other times, Mizner would lecture me about society's concept of fat in previous centuries or other cultures. I had to sit there and listen to him gas on about those famous eighteenth-century paintings of voluptuous women, with their cottage cheese thighs and buttocks. *Fuck all those cellulite-ridden bodies in those cloying paintings,* I'd think, and *Fuck the tribe in Africa where fatter is better.* What did any of this mean to me? To my culture? To sitting there bursting out of my clothes? To walking down a street and not having men turn their heads?

One day I made the mistake of telling Mizner that his doorman, Bob, drove me crazy, how he never recognized me. Mizner got all excited. He took the opportunity to tell me about another patient, a very successful businessman who felt slighted when his doorman didn't greet him with a proper hello or when a cabby failed to thank him for his tip. The patient struck me as the kind of asshole the city was more than amply populated with, self-important businessmen who think they are better than everyone else. But this was not Mizner's point at all. Rather, his patient suffered from low self-esteem, he said, which is why he needed so much validation from everyone, including the doorman and cabby.

I tried to picture this patient of Mizner's, but I didn't feel sympathetic and I didn't see myself as comparable, though Mizner was clearly telling the story for my benefit. I was meant to understand that Bob the Doorman was just doing his job, that my need for recognition was really about my neediness. And he seemed to be suggesting that I could just get rid of my low self-esteem like a frumpy old coat and replace it with a new, more stylish model.

"How many people do you suppose come through the building each day?"

I didn't answer.

"Each week?"

Silence.

"Do you realistically expect Bob to remember each and every one?"

Was I supposed to sympathize with Bob? I didn't

really want to torch him, but Dr. Mizner made me feel as if I were completely insane to think that his doorman should remember me, the great me. Then again, the deli guy near where I lived had figured out how I took my coffee after three visits.

Mizner sat there, stirring his unlit pipe in his mouth as if he were slowly sautéing something in there. He was actually waiting for an answer to his question. It wasn't rhetorical.

"How many people?" he repeated. "How many would you estimate?"

I didn't know how to answer. It was like being back in high school staring at a charmless teacher who has just asked the class the date of the Emancipation Proclamation. "People, I'm waiting." The room filling with a chalky silence.

I couldn't believe that my weekly rendezvous with the doorman was only about my lack of self-esteem, some inordinate desire to be recognized. But I could never win a round against Mizner. His mind was made up. Sometimes I'd try to accept his interpretation. I had read a great deal of Freud, and I was certainly aware of the central role that resistance played in therapy: the more I argued my position, the more likely that Mizner had touched a nerve. But with Mizner it started to feel like a zero-sum game. If I resisted, he was right. If I didn't resist, he was right. I always appeared irrational and he supremely rational.

Eventually it felt as if all my complaints were being managed with a fable or a story of another patient, some therapeutic parable to set me straight. I told Mizner about a guy who had asked me out, a guy I really liked. Sometime during our second dinner, I had confided that I was seeing a shrink. He told me he always thought he should see a shrink, too, and asked a lot of questions about it. I was convinced the date was a success, but he never called back and I was fairly crushed. Mizner responded by telling me about a patient of his who had been hospitalized. She apparently blurted out the whole story of her hospitalization to the first man she met upon being released.

"Do you think he ever called her?" Mizner tilted back in his chair.

I looked down.

"What's the point of the story?" Mizner asked, the stuffing from the split seam in his chair suddenly appearing sinister, mocking.

To me the woman seemed completely pathetic. I saw her spilling the worst details of her hospitalization to some unsuspecting guy. How was my situation equivalent? This woman, this former mental patient, was nothing like me. Nor could I place her in my movie pantheon, where even the most disturbed females were played by great beauties. Plus, if this were a movie, Dr. Mizner's patient could spill her guts and the guy would still love her. I wondered aloud how she landed the date in the first place (in my mind's eye, she was hideously fat, with stringy hair and plain clothes). But Mizner's only interest was whether I got the point, if I understood why the fellow never called back. A moron could get the point, but Mizner wouldn't drop it until I supplied the ending, until I answered his question. Did the guy ever call back?

On the side table next to my chair was an ashtray, a thick triangle shape with a pumpkin-orange glaze and tiny white flecks that looked like sperm. When I asked about its origin in one of our first sessions, Mizner told me that it was a gift from one of his patients. I understood it immediately to be mental hospital art. No one makes ashtrays or pot holders unless she's institutionalized. Now I imagined that the patient who blew her date was also the maker of the ashtray. I touched it. Imagined flinging it in Mizner's face.

During another session I complained to Mizner about a guy I knew from the library whom I was sort of seeing—we'd hang out together rather than have actual dates. Then one night he called at one in the morning and asked if he could come over. I was both annoyed and intrigued, and I said yes. We had sex, though when he left we both acted as if nothing happened. Then, for more than a week he wasn't at our usual spot in the library. He seemed to have disappeared. I felt frantic. I called and hung up at his dorm more times than I wanted to admit. Mizner tapped his teeth with his pipe as I told him the story. This was classic, he told me. The guy was testing me, finding out what kind of woman I was. If I would let him come over in the middle of the night and have sex with him, why should he make a proper date, why woo me? He told me about a patient, a very attractive woman who had been courted by a senior partner in her office for a long time. She finally accepted a dinner date with him and they wound up sleeping together that same night.

"Guess what happened?" Mizner asked.

"He never called back," I said, rolling my eyes.

"Bingo."

I told myself that Dr. Mizner was supplying the male point of view, which I sorely lacked, having grown up in a family of girls. I told myself he was right.

"And she is very thin," Mizner added.

food and loathing

I was meant to glean that attractive women can be rejected just as easily as women with weight problems. But I didn't really believe that. I was convinced that everything bad or disappointing or shitty that ever happened to me was the result of twenty or thirty or forty extra pounds. Dr. Mizner didn't share this view. I wondered what he would think if he could see me riding the M5 bus home from therapy each week, feeding my face with black-and-white cookies the size of plates from the deli near his office, wishing my stop would never come.

When I told him how hurt I felt if a woman friend canceled plans at the last minute to go out with a guy, Mizner would defend her, announcing with absolute authority that romantic love takes precedence over friendship. Always has, always will.

When I complained that my mother was always trying to fix how I looked, he told me that his own mother constantly complained about the length of his hair. Every time he saw her she'd remark on it, but Mizner would let the comments roll off his back "like water off a duck." And he asked why I couldn't try that.

When I complained that my parents' love felt contingent on my performance, on my successes, he explained that even babies have to coo and smile to get their parents to love them. "There is no such thing as unconditional love."

And when I cried that I was failing, that I couldn't finish a paper, that I was barely able to send away to graduate schools for applications, let alone apply, Dr. Mizner repeated his favorite story, the fable that came to characterize all our sessions and describe my life: the boy who cried wolf.

"You know the story," he would say, loudly repeating the best-known fable of all time of the boy who falsely called for help so many times that when he really needed help no one heeded. Sometimes he would adapt the story by using an example from his life, describing a fellow in his class at medical school, the most brilliant student, who always carried on that he wasn't prepared for an exam, which he would then ace. I tried to imagine Mizner as a young medical student, but I couldn't picture it.

In years to come I would encounter Freud's case of the Wolf-Man and his mysterious dream of the seven white wolves. As a child, I too had had a recurring dream involving a wolf—mine from the story of Little Red Riding Hood. In my dream the wolf was always positioned in the hall between my parents' bedroom and my own, rocking in a wooden rocker, the floor creaking under its weight. If I summoned the courage to peek through the crack in my door, I would spy the wolf's terrible teeth and gumline, mottled pink and gray. Though desperate to run to my parents, I knew I would be devoured, so I stayed alone in terror.

When I first read Freud's analysis of the Wolf-Man's dream, I was astonished to find so many parallels to my own dream, especially the young boy's paralysis in the face of the wolves. Freud took every detail of the Wolf-Man's dream and traced it to something real in the dreamer's life. Everything had significance—the number of wolves in the tree, their whiteness, their strange stillness. And I knew in a moment of absolute clarity that Mizner had been wrong, that my problem was not that of the boy in Aesop's fable. Rather, I was the boy who could not cry out even when there was a wolf. One child in our family had already died; who would be eaten next?

In my first year after college, I got pregnant after a disastrous one-night stand. When I told Mizner, he said it was impossible to tell only a week after having intercourse.

"I know I'm pregnant," I said.

"Impossible." He would have none of it.

Crying Wolf

"How can you be so sure?"

"Betsy, it's impossible to tell. You haven't even missed a period yet. The earliest you can get a pregnancy test is six weeks."

I just stared at him.

"I know," he said, "because my wife is pregnant."

That was all I needed to hear. Mizner's wife pregnant, sitting in their sunny kitchen with a book of baby names. Mizner's wife picking out a crib and colors for the nursery. Mizner feeling like the king of the world, making his wife round with child. Mizner pressing his ear to his wife's belly and listening for that oceanic sound.

"Why do you think you're pregnant?"

"I feel different."

"How?"

I couldn't answer. But everything about me—my skin, my breasts—felt different. My face looked different to me. I even smelled different. I didn't venture any of this to Mizner.

He asked me who the father was.

I had had a crush on Paul, a peripheral friend of some people I knew in college. One night we ran into each other at the Peppermint Lounge and made our way back to my apartment with Jim, a friend of his. We were already intoxicated but joked that the night was young. We smoked a joint, and Jim cut a few lines of coke. The two of them started moving their hips to Marvin Gaye's new album and then, in a rare moment of disinhibition, I joined in. At first it was fun—I was excited to have Paul over. But then Jim started grinding his hips into mine and making out with me. Paul drifted off into the bedroom. I hated the way Jim kissed, his tongue everywhere and pointy. I should have asked them to leave then; this was turning out all wrong. But I continued to make out with Jim, as if to show Paul that I cared as little for him as he did for me. Jim pinned me on my futon couch and put his hand down my pants. Paul had turned on the TV, and the sound of canned laughter blared out from the bedroom in brief, obscene belches over the music. Not knowing how to stop, I let Jim finish what I had so mistakenly let him start. I buried my head in the futon, hoping the blackness there would make the whole sordid scene go away. I'd made some very bad choices in the past, but nothing compared to the humiliation of this.

When I woke up the next morning, my apartment was trashed—beer bottles everywhere, cigarettes crushed out on the floor, the stereo needle repeating on a skip in the record. *Get up, get up, get up.* I ran to lock the door and fell in a heap in the corner behind it.

Crying Wolf

I couldn't tell Mizner about the experience. I couldn't bear to listen to anything he might say about my conduct. And god knows, if there was an Aesop's fable that he could summon, I didn't want to hear it.

I went to Planned Parenthood after four weeks and discovered that I was in fact pregnant.

"You see," I said, "I was right about being pregnant."

"It must be nice to know you're fertile."

That was all he said. Funny thing is, that question had never crossed my mind. I had never dreamed of having children, never imagined that my life would unfold in any conventional way, with a two-car garage and a husband. Still caught up in my own parental battles, I never imagined a child calling me "Mommy." Being pregnant wasn't about being fertile or having a child. I just knew that I did not want to be pregnant.

Two weeks later when I went to get an abortion, I was examined and sent home for being too small; the pregnancy wasn't advanced enough. Was this the great joke life would play on me? Finally I was too small for something.

To pass the time until I could have the abortion I took time off from my job, working in the library of the investment bank Morgan Stanley, where I fetched financial documents for type A men and women. After failing all my publishing interviews, I had taken the library job as a stopgap. It turned out I was a fairly efficient document retriever, and my boss was generous when I asked for the early vacation time. I decided to go to London for those weeks. It seemed easier to be in a different city in an altogether different country to wait. London was perfectly gray every day, there was no hint of sunshine to destroy my mood. I walked the streets during the day and went to a movie every afternoon and every night, sampling both the salted and the caramel popcorn.

Back in New York, I returned to the abortion clinic. Everyone in the waiting room was with a boyfriend or friend. One girl was with her mother. Why was I alone? My older sister and a friend from OA had offered to take me, and I had lied to each of them, saying someone else was coming. Sitting in that stuffy room with its shades of mustard furniture, I instantly regretted my decision. When the nurse practitioner asked if anyone was with me, I nearly broke down. She was concerned that I might feel weak, might pass out; it was important to have someone there. I assured her that a friend would take me home. When the cab dropped me off at my apartment, I was doubled over in pain and could barely get out. The driver impatiently threw the car into park and slumped over the wheel. Finally he turned around to see what was taking so long. And then, in a rare gesture of kindness, he jumped out and came around to help me.

"Why didn't you say you needed help?"

⌘

"Betsy, do you want to win?" Mizner would ask, lifting his eyebrows as if to emphasize how much fun winning was. I would stare at him in disbelief, then stupor. Win? *Win?* The word wasn't in my vocabulary. In the first place, anyone I might have construed as a "winner" was certainly some kind of asshole, like the cocky young guys at Morgan Stanley who actually believed they were masters of the universe.

"Do you want to win?" he'd repeat. "Do you?"

I started to check out during these inquisitions, a skill I had learned from my mother. I remember saying her name a hundred times, right in her face, and if she had that blank look in her eye, I could say it a hundred more. I knew she knew I was there. And I knew that eventually she would engage with me, but during those times it was as if she were in a trance. For me, willful tuning out took practice, but I learned how to disappear myself during those sessions, often lulled and calmed by the gentle warbling of the fat pigeons on the windowsill.

food and loathing

"Do you want to win?" That question again.

"I just want to cope" is what I finally managed to say.

⬥

During fall application season, two years out of college, Dr. Mizner bet me my pearl necklace that I would get into graduate school. In spring, the letters arrived. Stanford rejected me on a Tuesday. The rejection from Iowa arrived on Wednesday. On Thursday my so-called safety school, Brooklyn, bagged me. On Friday, feeling quite certain that Columbia would follow suit, I staved off despair by having dinner at the Second Avenue Deli and then attending the open poetry workshop at St. Mark's Church. I usually shared this Friday night ritual of pastrami and poetry with John, from my writers' group.

John, a first-generation American, was the first in his family to go to college. I always felt vaguely embarrassed around him, conscious that I had squandered my education while he was so earnest. I was always trying so hard to be cool. I remember him coming to a party and dancing and seeming very comfortable in his skin. He tried to get me to dance, but I pretended to be on a desperate search for a cigarette. I was thrilled when he first called to invite me to the poetry workshop. Between the time of his call and our meeting three nights later, under the yellow-and-pink sign of the Second Avenue Deli, I had fantasized a life for us along the lines of Sartre and Beauvoir.

The St. Mark's poetry workshop, which could have been dubbed the Deadbeat Poets Society, was a ragtag group of writers, mostly men in cowboy boots who carried their poems in their back jeans pocket and struck me as Sam Shepard imitators. One completely bald man, who reminded me of a sweet Uncle Fester without the turtleneck, always choked up when he read his poetry. A number of highly disheveled types had fairly impressive cases of body odor.

After the workshop John and I parked ourselves at a small table by the wall at the Cloister Café and yammered for hours about the people in the workshop, the teacher, the way one of the cowboy poets stormed out when no one understood his poem. We roared remembering his killer line, delivered with Dylanesque heat: *If you're scared of everything, babe, I'm scared of you.* Eventually I turned my attention to critiquing John's poems. The last one, "Love Poem," was dedicated to Miranda. There went Paris. I said I wouldn't critique the poem until he told me who Miranda was. He said he'd tell me afterward, didn't want to color my reading. I understood immediately that she wasn't an ex. After I finished my hasty critique John told me that she was his girlfriend. I pried for a few facts. She was a banker at a big, prestigious firm. She trekked all over the world and volunteered at a hospice. She had a Mensa IQ. I wagered that she did brain surgery in her spare time. Only the greatest restraint prevented me from asking if she was also a ballet dancer. It didn't matter—I knew her body was a lean and lifted thing of beauty.

The best night I had had in many months was unraveling before me. What had I been thinking? Of course he had a girlfriend. My bright, chatty, inquiring self collapsed into someone moody and aloof. John walked me partway home, west on the now nearly deserted Tenth Street. He kept talking about the workshop, about how great it was to be thinking about poetry in an active way instead of just studying it. He lit a cigarette for me, remarked on the way the light of the moon fell on the brick face of the building across the street. I kept my eyes on the pitted sidewalks. When he suggested we meet every Friday for dinner and the workshop, I was taken aback.

"What about Miranda?" I asked. More a taunt than a question.

"She works long hours."

Crying Wolf

I took myself in hand and decided his friendship was better than nothing. It had been a long time since I'd found a friend with whom I could talk about poetry and life. Everything John did was large: He loved opera, loved to talk all night, collected records and books by the thousands. He loved to cook and eat. He was a man unashamed of his appetites: for women, travel, experience. He amplified life. But his great love was books, and in this our solitary souls most deeply connected. He told me how as a young boy he hid out in the woods during lunch hour, saving his lunch money to buy books. I imagined him crouching like a refugee child, until it was time to rejoin his schoolmates, the coins in his hot hand growing oily and sharp.

I vowed to keep our new friendship completely platonic. Anyway, there was no way to compete with the woman he had described. I looked forward to Friday nights: our mutual love of high-cholesterol foods, the little dramas that unfolded each week at the workshop, but most of all the talk and cigarettes afterward at the Cloister Café.

John couldn't make it to the workshop the Friday of my graduate-school slaughter. I decided to go alone, telling myself that if rejection from the writing programs was enough to make me stop writing, then I didn't deserve to be a writer. I hadn't expected to get into Stanford or Iowa, but the Brooklyn rejection was a blow. I didn't even want to go there. I hadn't given any thought to a plan B, though my boss at Morgan Stanley kept encouraging me to get my master's in library science. She praised my ability for retrieving documents. The firm would even pay the tuition. Every time she brought it up, I imagined myself at three hundred pounds shelving books in the stacks of my hometown library.

I marched myself over to the deli that wet April night and was ushered to a small table near the kitchen. The waiter breezed over, all business. When I tried to speak, I could barely whisper my order.

"What is it, dear?" he said. "You're going to have to speak up." He tapped his ear to indicate a hearing aid. I noticed the tiny nest growing out of his ear and averted my gaze back to the menu. When I repeated my order, my voice cracked and my chin started to quiver.

He leaned in then and whispered, "Is it a fella? Didya break it up?"

"No, it's not that," I said.

"Then what?"

"I didn't get in to graduate school."

"A bright girl like you, that's gotta be a mistake."

I didn't know what to say. It was one of those moments when you wish that life were a musical and a kind waiter would break into song and make it all better.

"Now, what'll it be?" he asked, removing a tiny stub of a pencil from behind his ear.

"Matzo-ball soup," I said.

"That's better. Now, can you give me a little smile?"

I tried to look at him and smile, but I couldn't. This wasn't the first time a person who barely knew me had made some comment about smiling, how it doesn't cost anything, how my face wouldn't crack. It always shocked me that a complete stranger felt compelled to comment on my demeanor. I believed that one thing you were perfectly free to do in New York was walk around scowling. This wasn't the Have a Nice Day capital, this was a mean, cold city that didn't care if you lived or died. As far as I was concerned, looking happy was a liability, marking you as either a neophyte New Yorker or a tourist who's so busy being amazed by everything that she gets bonked with a brick or shoved in front of a subway train.

When a stranger called out to me to smile, I believed he was doing more than invading my person; he was launching an assault on everything I loved and held dear about my city. But that night, when the waiter asked me to smile, I really wanted to. I wanted to show him that I was a brave girl, but suddenly it was all too much. I felt nauseated. The smell inside the deli turned fetid, everything looked dull and greasy—the tabletop, the silverware, the waiter's face. I wanted to leave, to disappear. The waiter headed for the kitchen. I sat there like a lump. The rejection letters came back to me: *We regret to inform you . . . We appreciate the chance to have considered your application . . .* We think you suck.

When I finally got home that night, the letter from Columbia was standing in my mailbox. W*e are pleased to inform you . . .* Was it possible?

Suddenly, the idea of going to Columbia filled me with wild hope. All the young hot-shot analysts were leaving Morgan Stanley for MBA programs, and I too would be released. And as far as I was concerned, an MFA was the superior path. Just getting out of my cubicle at Morgan Stanley, leaving that airless, corporate environment with its dress code (no slacks, pantyhose required) was heaven enough.

Dr. Mizner wouldn't take the pearls he had bet me. Far more important than the bet was that he had been proved right. He was very pleased with himself. I couldn't pretend that I wasn't happy, too. But for Mizner this victory seemed to prove once and for all that I was the boy who cried wolf, that my problems and fears were all in my head. Which, of course, was why I was seeing a shrink in the first place.

Five

The Most of It

Men looked at me again. That spring before starting graduate school, I was attending OA meetings religiously and had been abstinent for nearly four months. I had dropped well below my fighting weight. I had deliberately picked a sponsor who terrified me. Carl had lost more than seventy-five pounds in OA. I had seen him at various meetings, and he had struck me as intense, with his shiny bald head and unblinking eyes. But it wasn't until his first anniversary, when he qualified and told the story of his life, that I fell under his spell. He spoke in a staccato monotone, unfolding a story of multiple addictions. In addition to food, Carl was addicted to sex, porn, and poppers. He was completely estranged from his family. When he came into the program he was in debt for more than $80,000, mostly from gambling, had lost a third job in three years, had no friends, and was nearly one hundred pounds overweight.

Few people took the program as seriously as Carl. It was clearly life or death for him. I convinced myself that working with Carl was what I needed. I knew there would be no charming him, no winning him over. If he agreed to take me on, I would have to get with the program. Even as every fiber in my body screamed for me to stay away, I nervously approached him after a meeting. He agreed to be my sponsor.

In the early weeks of our working together, when I was still slipping and sliding, Carl would take me for coffee after the meeting and stare at me in silence, his eyes bulging, while I fiddled with a Sweet'n Low packet. Then he would cock his head, smile broadly, and say, "How badly do you want it?" I knew he meant how badly did I want abstinence or getting with the program, but it sounded more sinister, sexual. Maybe if I hadn't heard him talk about the porn and poppers I wouldn't have thought that, but everything Carl said had edge, even the way he ordered his coffee, smiling too broadly at the waiter. I never knew what to say, but I knew that if I didn't supply the right answer, he would ask again and again. *How badly do you want it?*

I told myself that my discomfort was due to my inauthentic attitude, my lack of commitment and humility. I didn't really want to turn my will over to the care of god as I understood him, as the program suggested; I just wanted to be thin.

Carl believed that any deviation from the program, no matter how small, was a deliberate act of sabotage. "You're to call me every day at the same time with your food plan. Within the hour isn't good enough."

Chastened, I'd nod my head.

"You're to call in any food changes, no matter how slight."

"Okay."

"I mean it. You switch green beans for broccoli, I want to know about it. *Before.* Not after you've eaten it."

I nodded in assent. In those days, before cell phones, it was often difficult to find a working pay phone. I didn't see how substituting one vegetable for another could be such a big deal, but Carl insisted it could capsize my whole program.

food and loathing

"It isn't about the broccoli," Carl said, "it's about *turning it over.*"

"Turning it over" was a big concept in the program. I knew it had to do with will and control and ego; you were meant to put these things in god's hands, "to let go and let God." I wrote furiously in my journals of letting go, of turning it over, of letting my Higher Power help me. I wrote of my gratitude and the grace that came with back-to-back days of abstinence.

I went to meetings every day, both OA and AA, for Carl had convinced me that I had to be completely substance-free. No more pot, no more Percodan, my drug of choice. I loved the AA meetings. Half the people looked like Keith Richards, and one week I found myself sitting next to a well-known downtown rocker. When it was his turn to share, he talked about going into a tailspin when he couldn't find a valve for his motorcycle. He was incredibly boring, but because he was famous, we all listened intently.

I tried to tell myself that this abstinence was the real thing. I tried to pretend that the shedding of pounds was secondary to my devotion to working the program. I wanted to believe that there was a Higher Power; how else could I explain my newfound ability to stay abstinent, to fit into my size-eight jeans again? But in truth, the value of each day was still determined by how far I strayed from the gray sheet diet, not god. I had done everything Carl wanted for four months and had lost forty pounds, but as usual I had hit a wall with my Higher Power. I told Carl I was afraid I was going to blow it. Carl had an answer for this spiritual dilemma. Pray, he said. Get on your knees and pray.

My knees would not bend when I went to the side of my bed that night. The only time I could summon any feeling of god was in synagogue during the most sacred of prayers, the *Alenu*. I loved that moment when the entire congregation bowed its collective head. It wasn't just the bowing, it was the music swelling and every face in the great sanctuary lifting. In that moment I would sense, in spite of all my disbelief, that life was precious. That ancient music with its heavy golden tones worked through me. To kneel seemed to me sacrilege, and though I stood by my bed hearing Carl's awful ordinances—*How badly do you want it?*—I was not willing to kneel.

At our next meeting, I told Carl that I couldn't do it and he shook his head in disappointment. I promised I would try again. But I could not summon any faith. When presented with the idea of god, I'd think of my little sister and how her loss rendered the world godless for my mother. I was four when Barbara died and had no real memory of her. Once, during one of my many scavenging forays into my mother's things, I came across a packet of photographs. One was of a little girl with spiky hair and sweetly drooping eyes. She was still in diapers and hanging on to the edge of an ottoman, taking what must have been her first steps. I couldn't place her, so I turned to the next: a picture of me and the same little girl on my parents' bed. I'm looking at her with what appears to be curiosity and she is grinning for the camera. I put the photos away quickly, as if I had been caught looking at a hidden stash of *Playboy* magazines.

⌘

"I can't believe you'd leave a job like this to work at a camp," my father said after seeing the Morgan Stanley offices. He had come to the city to take me out to dinner, and I had given him a brief tour. Once he had seen the trading floor and all the framed tombstones that lined the reception area, boasting their multimillion-dollar deals, he was even more consternated that I'd walk away from an opportunity he would have given his eyeteeth for.

"I'm going to graduate school in the fall anyway. What difference does it make if I leave two months early?"

The Most of It

Our steaks arrived. We liked them well done. We liked and disliked all the same foods. We were very similar: compulsive, capable, well liked, overweight. I hated disappointing my father in anything. His fantasy of my life at Morgan Stanley was full of career and marriage opportunities. He seemed to think that I was in the hot-shot analyst training program with all the Young Turks gunning for Wall Street. Didn't he see that I worked in the *library,* with people who brought tomato soup in a Thermos for lunch. I have never seen a sight so sad as a grown man eating from a plastic container at his desk, his tie hoisted over one shoulder, his eyes trained on the middle distance as he solemnly chews. Morgan Stanley had neither the glamour nor the romantic possibilities my father conjured, yet he wouldn't let up. This camp thing was a mistake, a waste of time.

"Daddy, what difference does it make? I'm leaving anyway."

"You're running away. You're too old to be a camp counselor."

"It's more than a counselor. I'm running the arts and crafts program. Why did I study pottery all those years?"

"For fun. This is an opportunity. Do you realize what the name Morgan Stanley means to the world?"

"Assholes."

My father didn't like my joke and responded by sawing into his steak.

"You don't know what you're throwing away," he finally said, wiping the fringe of his mustache before throwing his napkin on the table as if surrendering the flag.

My father wasn't the only one who thought working at a camp was a bad idea. Carl told me I didn't have enough abstinence to leave the city and meetings; I would be making a big mistake if I took the summer job. His warning was even more fearsome than my father's disapproval. Somehow, though, I defied them both.

∞

I had one hurdle to clear before the camp season began: I was to be maid of honor at my older sister's wedding. I spent a day in Boston with my sister and my mother shopping for a dress. The inevitable tears and fighting from that day have long faded, but I will never forget the look on my mother's face when she effortlessly zipped me into a fitted size-six pink chiffon dress. I had done it! I had transformed my body once again into the svelte shape of the girl who had gone off to Israel, and I felt the approval ratings as surely as a presidential candidate accepting his party's nomination.

The Most of It

The only problem being that I was no longer that girl. My head wasn't full of hope and possibility, looking forward to that first kiss. All the innocence of that summer had been squandered on bad liaisons, consumed by self-hatred. Now, though I had crawled my way back to this weight, I knew it was a precarious victory at best. Still, I received constant attention for my new figure from friends and relations who had gathered for the wedding, many of whom didn't even recognize me. I heard myself telling people that I was starting Columbia in the fall to study writing. I painted a bright picture of my summer running the pottery program at an exclusive girls' dance camp. It all sounded ideal, but for the constant tape looping through my brain: *You're just one bite away. You're just one bite away.*

After the rehearsal dinner I went with some of the bridal party to Toad's, a New Haven bar. I was standing by the dance floor when a tall, cute guy pretended to accidentally bump my hip. We started talking and dancing, and he moved his head in a sweet Gumbyish way. We walked outside, smoked a couple of cigarettes, and found our way to his car. Inside it we started kissing, his breath warm and beery. He took me to the bowling alley where he worked. It was after hours, and the place was empty, the lanes awash in green light. He dropped some coins into the jukebox, and we slow-danced. He was more gentle than any of the guys I had been with. He kept holding and stroking my face. He wanted to take it slow, but I urged him on. His adoration made me uncomfortable. We had sex on one of the red leatherette couches behind the lanes, and he went on and on about my body, how beautiful it was. I was confused and disgusted by his affection, and I became mean and aggressive. He was turned on by this, and we went at it again in a frenzy of body contact that verged on pain. Suddenly noticing how strong he was, I briefly imagined myself as Diane Keaton in *Looking for Mr. Goodbar,* then felt self-conscious and afraid. The bowling alley no longer looked surreal and beautiful. *Where was I and who was this guy?*

He sensed the change in me and asked what was wrong. I told him I wanted to go home. I frantically pulled my pants and bra on, looked around for my shirt. He was baffled by my sudden about-face, tried to calm me down. I kept saying I wanted to go home, and, nice guy that he was, he dressed quickly and fished his shoes out from under the banquette. Except for giving him directions to my parents' house, I remained silent for the entire car trip. I couldn't even say good night when we finally got there and I bolted up our driveway.

The next day at the wedding I led the procession

down the aisle at B'nai Jacob. As the organ began to play, I felt everyone's eyes on me, heard the whispers of approval and astonishment at my figure. I could barely walk after the night before. This was the first wedding for our family, and my mother was wildly anxious for everything to go well and look right. She had, in fact, done a beautiful job. The great room was transformed, awash in flowers beneath a huppah laden with vines and white lilies. Even the Sweet'n Low packets were fitted into decorative envelopes. God most certainly was in the details that day.

As we stood on the bima in the sanctuary of our temple to witness this marriage, I tried to remember the face of the man I had been with the night before. All I could summon were his shoulders. I told myself that this wedding, my sister, the peach-colored carpet rolling through the aisles, was all someone else's dream.

After the ceremony the photographer arranged us for the classic family shot. Everyone in our family was heavy in varying degrees, from massively obese to chubby, and as we lined up across the steps of the bima, the collective girth was ample. My uncle Phil joked that we looked like the Jack La Lanne "before" photo. Everyone broke up.

food and loathing

The first thing I did when I arrived at camp was look for an OA meeting. I couldn't find one anywhere on the Cape and went to an AA meeting instead. It was nothing like those held in Manhattan, more closely resembling a social club for senior citizens than anything else. When I told them I was in Overeaters Anonymous, they laughed. They had never heard of it, couldn't understand how a few cookies could hurt you. I spent most of my energy staying away from the doughnuts and watery coffee at the snack table. It was the equivalent of my bringing a six-pack to their meeting. Even more challenging was the ride back to camp, with every kind of fast-food franchise beckoning from the roadside.

In the first two weeks of camp I busied myself getting to know the girls in my bunk, setting up the pottery shed, and jogging the two-mile loop around the quarry. I was strong and fast, I had cut my hair very short, and sometimes I pretended I was a boy as I sprinted down the camp driveway to the soft dirt path. Most mornings the mist would be rising around my ankles, and sometimes a fat raccoon on a large rock would give me a great scare.

The girls were twelve and thirteen, most of them from Manhattan, most from broken homes. They seemed more savvy than I could ever hope to be, yet they sought my attention, my approval. One girl in particular, Zoe, was always asking me questions about boyfriends and sex. She was a stunning girl with light green eyes and olive skin. Her hair was thick and curly, and she moved like a great cat, her limbs longer than she knew what to do with.

"My father's girlfriend has a tattoo on her shoulder," she said when we first met, and pulled her T-shirt down to expose her own bare shoulder.

"She gave me this ring," and cocked her thumb for me to see the silver band. "Do you like it?"

"It's cool," I said, never having seen a thumb ring before.

She announced one morning that her mother was frigid. "That's why my father left her, you know."

"That sounds kind of personal," I said, not wanting the other girls to pursue the meaning of sexual dysfunction.

"Are you?"

"What?"

"Frigid."

"What do you think?" I said, employing my usual evasion.

"What is frigid, anyway?" Zoe asked, shaking her curls around her face.

Another night, when I was settling them all into bed, she asked how many guys I'd slept with.

food and loathing

"Zoe, that's none of your business."

"Two? Ten? Strike that. How many girls have you slept with?" At this, she laughed so hard she bounced off the cot onto the floor. She sat there in her T-shirt and underwear laughing hysterically and continued with her questions—had I ever been fist-fucked? did I have a vibrator? been in a three-way?—until she had all the girls cracking up, while I stood there astonished to hear her laundry list—did I rim? did I sixty-nine? what about anal? The next night she topped her performance by straddling an enormous watermelon and rocking back and forth on it, screaming, "I'm coming, I'm coming."

I didn't reveal my private life to Zoe or to the others, and this strategy proved effective. The less I said, the more they confided in me. The pottery shed became a place where the girls could hang out and relax. I'd look the other way if they wanted to smoke or spin each other around on the wheels. These girls were dancers; they would know their own share of agony soon enough. The pressure to stay tiny and lithe was going to crack at least a few.

Sometimes, after shutting down the pottery shed at the end of the day and wandering back up to my bunk, I'd see a few girls on the outdoor stage. I'd stay back and watch them rehearse in their sweats and leggings, bend-ing as easily as marionettes. They would twirl in that beautiful late afternoon light, the brass sunlight suffusing their perfect movements, dancing a *pas de deux* or stretching into an arabesque.

Watching them, I thought about my own attempts at ballet at Miss Stodell's New Haven studio when I was five and six. I remembered how chubby I looked and how embarrassed I was to discover that I was the only girl wearing underpants beneath her leotard. At eight, I discovered pottery, which I was good at and loved. When I was older and making fairly good-sized bowls and cylinders, one of my teachers commented that all my pots were a little bottom-heavy. I became convinced that just as owners are said to resemble their dogs, so did I resemble my salad bowl. After that I smashed every pot I didn't consider perfect. I told myself that I cared only about the process, that saving pieces was of no interest to me. But smashing those bottom-heavy pots, those effigies of myself, hurling them against the great brick wall behind the pottery studio, gave me something concrete to destroy.

Big trouble arrived in the form of the director's daughter a few weeks into the summer. Teena was a recovering junkie, home after many years of living in the Castro and other sexy-sounding places. Her jet-black hair looked as if it had been cut with a cleaver. She had tattoos and scars all over her arms, from cutting and from what looked like cigarette burns. There was a rumor that the knot of scar at her throat was from the time she tried to hang herself in the big dance barn. I didn't believe it, but I could no longer walk into the barn without glancing up at the high rafters, imagining Teena hanging there in a white sack dress. She smoked Marlboros nonstop and took me riding through the woods, showing me the hidden quarries, places I never would have found myself. We got high together. She told me stories of her using days, and I listened like a rapt camper sitting by the fire. She told me she just smoked pot now, and I idiotically believed her. Two weeks later she was rushed to a hospital, the emergency lights of the ambulance washing the bunk walls with its hideous red pulse.

The camp director insinuated that I was mixed up in Teena's overdose. She knew that I had a problem with addiction because she had let me take the camp van to go to the AA meetings. I was too embarrassed to tell her that I was going because of food, not booze or drugs.

The next day it was my turn to drive the girls into town for a free afternoon. I kept saying the serenity prayer about accepting the things I could not change, but the minute after I dropped off the girls, I raced to a McDonald's on the highway and bought a Quarter Pounder, large fries, and a chocolate milkshake. It all went down before I could taste a single bite. Still buzzing from the milkshake, I raced to the next fast-food place and started over. I bolted back to meet the girls, my heart pounding as if I'd pulled a bank heist, and found that I had arrived at the designated meeting place too early. To calm myself I bought coffee and a bran muffin and waited for the girls to wander back from their shopping. I knew that to the world I looked the same, but inside I was seized with terror. I was certain that in just a single binge I had put forty pounds back on. All I could think of was where and when I could get more food. Carl was right. The floodgates had opened.

Driving the girls back to camp, I pulled over to a Dunkin' Donuts and bought two boxes of Munchkins, one for the girls in the car and one supposedly for the girls in my bunk (I planned to stash the doughnuts in the pottery shed and consume them myself). In my addled state I pulled out from the Dunkin' Donuts without looking carefully. The car speeding by had to swerve out of my way, and the driver leaned on his horn and gave me the finger à la Dennis Hopper in *Easy Rider*. My heart was racing as the girls bounced around in the van like a bunch of caged monkeys stimulated by the excitement of our near miss. I kept replaying the moment, hearing the blare of the horn and seeing the outstretched hand with the middle finger. I convinced myself that I should not be driving these girls. I told myself I had to leave, had to get back to New York, to the meetings and Carl.

That night I left a message for John, and he returned the call at camp. It was my great luck that his sales route for a small publisher had taken him to Cambridge, maybe ninety miles away. When he told me he could swing through in a couple of days and pick me up, take me back with him to New York, I made my decision to leave. I could barely face the girls as I bid them farewell. Zoe seemed more excited than saddened by my sudden departure. She hung around while I packed, jumping from one bed to another.

"Please tell me who he is," she begged. "I won't tell a soul."

"He's just a friend," I soberly said.

"A friend, or a *friend*?" She drew out the second word.

"Just a friend," I said, though I secretly wished for more.

"You've done him, I can tell," she said and plopped down on my bed.

"Zoe, you don't know everything."

"Yes, I do. Even my stepmother can't believe how intuitive I am."

"You are that," I said, emptying my last cubby.

"Then I'm right?"

"You never know."

Zoe nodded her head vigorously to prove that she was right, and I liked that she had imagined a full-blown love affair for me with John.

When John arrived, I went to say goodbye to the director. She angrily scribbled a check for the month I had worked. I didn't want to take it, but she shoved it in my bag and walked away without saying goodbye. I had never forfeited on any commitment, but I told myself I was doing the responsible thing, if only to make myself feel better. I shuddered to think what might have happened if I had run the van off the road and killed or hurt a single one of those beautiful girls.

John was the only friend I had ever asked for help. He seemed to relish the role of arriving at the camp, my white knight, albeit in a Ford Taurus. He made the trip home take longer than it needed to, and I regaled him with the camp fiasco, the girls, the quarry. He described a calamitous affair in Kent, Connecticut, with a woman who might be pregnant with his child.

We stopped at Rye Playland on the drive back to the city. We spread out towels and lay on the gritty sand and talked for hours. I was wearing an electric-blue one-piece suit with white piping and a fairly plunging neckline. I was strong and muscular from running and from lifting and wedging so much clay. At one point I felt John looking at my breasts, and I knew that despite my binge I still looked good, but I could have swum the ocean and back sooner than make a move for him.

When we finally came to the George Washington Bridge, the reverie began to fade. John would return to work the next day, and I would start school in a month. I had already moved out of my one-bedroom apartment on Fourteenth Street and into a tiny room in an artist's apartment in Inwood, a little-known neighborhood above Harlem and Washington Heights in the northernmost reaches of the city. I liked the spartan feeling of my corner room: all it held was a single bed, a desk, a chair, a lamp, a phone, an ashtray, and a small chest of drawers in the closet. I hung a poster of Diane Arbus's famous photograph of twins in matching outfits. Everything about the sisters is identical but for one girl's drooping eyes, which seemed to embody everything that was unfair in the world.

John dropped me off and took a quick peek inside. The room was barely big enough for both of us, the single bed casting a monastic eye over us.

"Are you going to be okay here?"

"Yeah," I said.

We awkwardly kissed and hugged, moving left, then right, like two boxers. Then he left.

I entered the Columbia campus that first day through the great black wrought-iron gates on 116th Street and Broadway. As I made my way up the stairs in Dodge Hall, I quickened my pace in an effort to gain confidence, only to take a shattering fall, my knapsack and pocketbook shooting off in opposite directions. I told myself that falling down was a good thing, a humbling thing. I often spoke such nonsense to myself, offering lines about humility from the program to ameliorate humiliation, trying to understand everything as part of some higher plan or purpose.

The centerpiece of the MFA program was the workshop, the two-hour class during which we sat around a table with a well-known poet and critiqued the work of our classmates. I had been assigned to Denis Johnson's workshop. I couldn't believe my luck. I worshiped Johnson. Any writer who spent time in downtown AA meetings was aware of his work. He had dedicated his first novel, *Angels,* to "H.P. and to those who have shared their experience, strength, and hope." We all knew H.P. stood for Higher Power. Johnson's first book of poetry, *The Incognito Lounge,* struck me as both brutal and tender, full of self-loathing and transcendent passages about delivery from pain. I fantasized that being in the program would endear me to Johnson, that we would connect on some spiritual plane. I'd turn him on to the cool downtown meetings, and we'd have coffee afterward in my favorite café and talk about poetry long into the night. All of this might have been possible had I been able to open my mouth and speak in his presence. The man was unbelievably sexy, dark, and tortured. His voice was a low motor. Between feeling completely inadequate among my fellow students and awestruck by Johnson, I sat in those workshops staring out from behind my big glasses like a goldfish in the wrong bowl.

Johnson, it turned out, wasn't much more comfortable. Teaching at Columbia seemed to be an excruciating experience for him. He could barely bring himself to comment on the poems we offered and usually sat at the table in silence. Sometimes he looked as if he were trying to pull up something from the dregs of his being to say to us eager sardines, but few words ever came out. Some of the students went to the director of the program to complain, but I admired his silence, his discomfort. I was convinced that his was the only honest response to the student writing before him. The fact that he wouldn't pander, offer any false hope, or comment for the sake of it struck me as pure. We all knew, on some level, how stupid and phony it was to be studying poetry writing, to be paying $20,000 to learn something that shouldn't need schooling.

I forced myself to hang out in the student lounge after workshops, but after a while I found it too painful to stand there rereading the bulletin board for the thousandth time. It was obvious that cliques had quickly formed and that certain groups headed off to certain bars. I was desperate to go along, but usually I ran off, pretending I had somewhere more important to be—and sometimes it was so. I was still trying to get to a meeting every day, and I convinced myself that I had to keep working my program. Except that I was starting to "play with my food" as Carl called it. And rather then confess to him that I was slipping, I had started to lie.

Before too long I went on a binge like the one at

camp, and soon after that the whole cycle started again. That fall I binged a couple of times a week. My size six went to eight and then to ten. I was still trying to pretend that I could get myself back under control. I was too afraid of the consequences of telling Carl, so I confided in Bettina, a woman in OA who struck me as someone I could trust. She seemed cooler than most of the people in the program, and I was dazzled by her thinness. Her long red hair seemed to contain all the henna in lower Manhattan, and she was a genius with thrift-store finds. We had read Johnson's poems together at a small dark café in the West Village, and she was impressed that I was studying with him. When I told Bettina that I was slipping, she became very grave, as if I'd told her I'd been fired from my job or was getting a divorce. At first she distanced herself from my contamination. Then she turned empathic, taking my hand and closing her eyes. She said she would pray for me. I wanted to strike her.

Another woman in the program, Brigid, was more understanding, but that was because she never stayed abstinent for more than a few days either. Brigid told me about her illustrious past as part of Andy Warhol's Factory, but after dangling a juicy story, she would abruptly change the subject. None of it meshed with her image now, in her Ralph Lauren polo shirts, crisp slacks, and

Belgian slippers. When she invited me to her apartment, I was struck by how prim and formal everything was: a shelf of silver-framed photographs of herself as a little girl with bows in her hair, her parents with Ronald Reagan, dogs past. She had two little designer dogs to whom she spoke as if they were small children.

Brigid kept no food in her fridge, which was filled instead with Perrier and foil-covered tins of dog food. She had laquer boxes filled with cigarettes and lighters almost too heavy to lift. She had a pixie's smile and a truck driver's laugh, and so long as we were both slipping and sliding in the program, we offered each other our compromised company. Years later I read about Brigid and discovered who she had been in Warhol's world. She had let him film her obese naked body, using it to make art, flaunting her weight. Her father had been president of the Hearst Corporation, and it occurred to me that she had grown up in the most privileged and pressured world imaginable, especially when it came to appearances. When Andy Warhol died, I thought of her again and wondered if she had been liberated or exploited by their work. We were friends, but the boat was leaky. Abstinence seemed like a life raft—staying on was a delicate balance between helping others and saving yourself.

Another friend in the program, Deena, confided

details of her childhood and the incest she had suffered at
the hands of her father, a wealthy and prominent New
York real estate man. She had been abstinent for almost a
year and had lost a lot of weight. But instead of bringing
her happiness, it left her vulnerable. The more pounds
she lost, the closer she came to the central trauma of her
life, which was threatening to capsize her small person.
She told me that lots of heavy women are victims of sexual, physical, or verbal abuse. She made me think about
my own father and our incestuous relationship with
food. Away from the censorious glare of my mother, we
had been binge buddies, sharing movies and junk food.
We were in it together. Did I betray him every time I lost
weight?

By November I was back in my size-fourteen jeans, and I
felt myself suffocating in their tightness. I wondered what
I looked like as I faced Dr. Mizner each week. I wanted to
disappear or take my place with the pigeons on the ledge.
I wanted to hurl myself out the window. I tried to imagine
the shattering of glass, the parachute my coat would make
as it briefly billowed in the air current before I plummeted
and collapsed in the air shaft below.

Dr. Mizner finally broke the silence. "Betsy, what are you thinking?"

His voice awakened me as if from a hypnotic state. When I looked at him, he no longer looked familiar. I knew I was all alone there, and I started to cry. I wiped my cheeks with my hand. Mizner gestured toward the Kleenex box. I refused to take so much as a tissue from him.

"Betsy, what is it that you want me to say?"

"Why don't you tell me about the boy who cried wolf again?"

"Betsy, what are you looking for here?"

How could I answer that question? What *wasn't* I looking for?

"I can't help you unless you tell me what you need."

At this I lost it. "I'm gaining all this weight. I can't stop bingeing. I'm a freak at school. I want to kill myself. You tell me I'm the boy who cries wolf. Where does that leave me? Where the *fuck* does that leave me?" And then I buried my face in my hands.

When I looked up again, Mizner was smiling. Not a big smile, a canary smile.

"Betsy," he said, "I'm sorry that I'm not in as much pain as you. I know you'd like me to be. But that is not how it works."

I started skipping sessions after that. The bingeing became a near-daily occurrence. Sometimes I'd walk the eighty blocks from the Columbia campus to my apartment in Inwood, stopping at every deli and bodega to replenish my supply of sweet and salty foods, eating all the chips and fried plantains and doughnuts I could manage. Home in my little room I'd curl up on the bed, doubled over in pain. If the phone rang I wouldn't answer it. I had developed a terrible phobia around the phone. No matter how lonely I felt, I'd let the phone ring thirty times without answering. I didn't yet have an answering machine, and I had developed a steel will about not picking up a ringing phone. On a couple of occasions my roommate poked her head in, trying to figure out why I wasn't answering the phone. She'd cock her head and make a question with her face.

"Do you know the phone is ringing?" she'd finally say as I stared at her and let the phone ring.

"Yes."

"Okay," she'd say, moving back from the door.

My roommate and I had stopped making any pretense of friendliness. One morning, as I left the apartment for school, I glimpsed her at her easel, wearing a huge straw hat. What an asshole—who the hell did she think she was, Vincent van Gogh?

Some days later when she wasn't home I sneaked into her studio. I admired the way she arranged tiny rows of blue glass and shells. She had a marvelous way of organizing textures and shapes into patterns, and I envied everything about her little world; even the brushes fanned out in a jar of turpentine looked exquisite. Then I saw the painting she had been working on: it was of herself wearing a straw hat. She had been working on a self-portrait that day; the hat was a prop. She wasn't pretending to be at Arles, or maybe she was, but the canvas was beautiful. It captured her dark eyes and angular features. She had perfectly re-created the weave of the straw hat, and I stood transfixed by the intricate patterns of brush strokes. My nose felt hot, my eyes began to sting with the gathering tears. I wanted to cry, wanted to smash all her canvases. Once again I had made my world a very small place, and I didn't want to live there. I grabbed my jacket and ran out to the park.

Fort Tryon Park was just blocks from the apartment. The Cloisters is there, home to the Metropolitan Museum's collection of medieval and Renaissance art. That fall I spent countless hours walking through the Gothic architecture and admiring the floor-to-ceiling tapestries, reading and writing in the outdoor courtyard next to an espaliered pear tree. Forced up the wall's face like the arms of a menorah, the tree's gray branches seemed to understand the sacrifice of freedom for beauty.

I knew every inch of the park, but I gravitated toward a small bridge at one of its hilly peaks that looked over the river to the New Jersey Palisades. As the traffic flushed through the Henry Hudson Parkway, I'd gaze across the wide river and hear strains of a stupid jingle from my childhood, advertising the Palisades Amusement Park: "Come on over. Swings all day and after dark. Come on over."

When I ran away from my roommate's self-portrait, I went straight for the overpass and nearly collapsed on the bench there. Why hadn't I bought some m&m's or something? The truth was, I was too embarrassed to visit the bodega near my apartment. They always said "Gracias" and smiled a lot, but I invented all kinds of judgments, imagining how they must have gossiped about me, the fat white girl who buys too much chocolate. I smoked a couple of cigarettes. The nicotine helped. The sound of the traffic helped. I got up to look over the edge. The drop was breathtaking. The image of my coat in midair came back to me. I saw myself fall in slow motion, the coat turning and folding in on itself like great black wings. Scared, I sat down. I went back to the apartment and wrote a poem entitled "Self-Portrait."

⌘

During the first weeks of December I visited that perch high above the Hudson almost every day. At that point I was easily back up to 170 pounds. I couldn't close my coat. I stopped going to meetings, I stopped seeing Dr. Mizner. I did attend classes, but I spoke to no one and no one spoke to me. I'd walk to and from the campus, eating, smoking, then visiting my secret spot, looking out at the cold river, the jagged cliffs. I'd go back after class and sit for hours, trying to gather what I would have called courage.

During the last week of classes that semester, I received a note in my mailbox to see Meena, the department secretary. I was convinced I was going to be asked to leave the program, and I felt relieved. I couldn't believe I was still attending. I went into the office feeling deeply ashamed of my appearance. Meena was a beautiful Indian woman whose eyes and voice were rich pools of kindness.

"Sit down," she said and touched the chair beside her desk.

I was aware of how enormous my thighs looked when I sat. I was afraid my coat was stained or dusted with crumbs from the junk food I'd been eating. I kept my eyes on the ground.

"What's wrong?" she said.

"Meena," I said, "I have to quit the program. I can't do it."

"But, Betsy," she said, "do you know why I wanted to see you?"

"To ask me to leave?"

"No." She laughed. "You're so silly. Your poem 'Self-Portrait' has won the Academy of American Poets second-place prize! We wanted to tell the winners first before we announced it." She leaned over to hug my stiff body. Then she held me by the shoulders and looked into my eyes. "This is good news, you know."

I looked at Meena, and she was still smiling with the good news.

"You cannot leave the program. Come on."

At home that night I wolfed down a combo plate of ribs, eggroll, and fried rice from the local Chinese take-out, Main Lung. I wanted to ask for extra duck sauce, but I was afraid of looking like a pig in front of the lithe girl who always took my order.

I made it through the holidays, overdosing on movies. I went to a few meetings, though not my usual ones, where I might run into Carl or others I knew.

The Most of It

Instead I found meetings in parts of town where no one knew me, sat in the back row, kept to myself. At one meeting an announcement was made about a woman who had checked into South Oaks Mental Institution and would welcome calls of support. I took down the number, even though I didn't know the woman and was not about to call.

I returned to school in the second week of January and tried to put a good face on things. But within days I was backsliding, bingeing. I walked through some of Harlem's most desolate streets, hoping to meet the danger the place was famous for.

On the phone my mother could tell I wasn't in great shape. Though I tried to hide it from her, she could always read my mood swings as if she had special radar, as if we were still connected. She knew from the first syllable I uttered over the phone whether I was up or down. Even when I tried to hide my depression with chirpy calls, she could detect the thin veneer. Part of me wanted to run home that winter, especially when I heard the concern in my mother's voice, but I was determined not to run back there.

"Can I come in for a day of shopping?" she offered when my voice sounded thin, hopeless. "Or I could pick you up at the train if you want to come home," she said, though I sensed she didn't really want my thick, stubborn body there. "Betsy, please just tell me what I can do."

"Nothing. I'm okay."

"Are you sure? Maybe I should call Dr. Mizner."

"No, don't do that. Please." I didn't want her to know that I hadn't seen him in weeks. "I'll figure something out. Really. Don't worry. I just need to get to a meeting."

She probably thought I needed medication from my days with Dr. Parker. I insisted that it was about food, that if I could get abstinent I would be fine. I was just convincing enough, or insistent enough, or, like an addict, deceptive enough, to get my way.

"Okay," she said. "Just promise to call in a day or so."

◦◦◦

January 26 was my father's birthday. I forgot, didn't send a card or call. In midmorning I went up to my spot and sat for a while. It started to snow. I don't know how much time passed; but eventually a fine dusting covered everything. I walked over to the thick concrete ledge and wrote my name in the snow. I lifted my leg to see how hard it would be to get up onto the ledge, then hoisted myself up with some effort, my arms and legs straddling the ledge. My heart was pounding with the effort. I felt the vibration of the traffic thrum through my body. Cars whooshed past with the pull of a vacuum. I held on tighter. *Let go,* the voice in my head urged. *Just let go.* But I held on. Every time a pack of cars raced by below, my body shuddered and I clutched the wall even harder. I wanted to cry out then, in frustration and desperation, but nothing came. *Just let go.* I rolled back off the ledge to the ground and stumbled backward to the safety of the bench. As I grabbed anxiously inside my pocket for a cigarette, I dropped my lighter. When I turned around to retrieve it, something moved in the bushes. Was I imagining it? A small man stepped out from the bushes, his erect penis in his hand, his expression that of a naughty boy.

How long had he been watching me? Had he seen me climb on the wall? I was flooded with shame and confusion. He stepped toward me. I took off running with all my might, never looking back until I got to the street, across it, and into my building.

Back in my room, I was soaked with sweat. What had happened? What was I doing? I found the phone number of the hospital that I copied down at the meeting a few weeks earlier, as if I had known all along that it was for me. When someone answered, I started crying hysterically about what had just happened. I was put on hold and finally a nurse came on the line. I was calmer by then. The woman asked if I had insurance, and I told her I was a student at Columbia. She told me to call the school's health services.

The health service nurse asked me to come down right away, so I took a subway to the campus and found my way to the psych floor of the health services building. After telling my tale to the doctor there, I was instructed to go to Columbia's eating disorders unit in midtown. Did I need someone to go with me? No, I could get there myself.

At the midtown branch I met with a woman who looked like Joan Baez and who, after taking down my story, said she wanted to talk with Dr. Mizner. This scared me. Even though I hadn't seen him in a month and he had never so much as called to see how I was, I felt as if I had tattled on him. I was also afraid he would tell her I was the boy who cried wolf. I begged her not to call him. She removed the chopstick from her loose bun, letting her hair fall around her shoulders.

"You're in serious shape and we need to make a strategy. It would help me to talk with your psychiatrist." As she said this, she swept her hair back up into a fresh bun and speared it with the chopstick in one graceful movement. "So I'd really like to call."

"Okay."

"Do you have his number?"

I reached into my backpack and found that all I had was my wallet and some loose papers and candy wrappers.

"I forgot my address book," I said, hoping this meant she wouldn't call. She picked up the receiver and dialed information, pressing the numbers with her thumb, a detail I found myself weirdly fixated on. She excused herself to make the call and returned to tell me that one bed was available at Columbia Presbyterian Hospital—the psych ward. As it was late on a Friday afternoon, she explained, I really should take it. There really weren't too many other options. I didn't want to go and I didn't not want to go. I told her that even though I had been going to the bridge for a couple of months, I hadn't really gotten close to jumping. It's true I was trying to make myself do it, but I never could.

She shook her head. "Don't you see, sweetie? It's just too close."

Again I protested. I told her about the poetry prize, as if to say, see, I *am* the boy who cried wolf. She wasn't having any of it.

"You shouldn't have to come that close."

She asked if I needed help getting to the hospital.

No, not me, don't need any help, I can do it myself. According to family mythology, I could, as a four-year-old, keep a carload of adults waiting while I insisted on tying my own shoes. I had gotten an abortion by myself. I would check into the hospital by myself. It's amazing I didn't give birth to myself.

Outside, I dreamed of fleeing the city, running away. I wanted to see John. I missed him terribly and fantasized that we would run away together, that he could take me on a long detour from my life.

~

The emergency room was a filthy place, crowded with alcoholics, drug addicts, stab victims, and screaming children. The wait to check in was interminable. The longer I sat in that squalid, overheated room, chilled by blasts of air that came in with the gurneys, the more desperate I became. I felt a piece of paper in my pocket and fished it out. It was the last poem our teacher Richard Howard had given us to study, titled "The Most of It," by Robert Frost. Did he mean you had to make the most of things? Or was this all there was? *The least of it,* I thought. *I have made the least of my life.*

The admitting doctor was a pert, clipped professional. She wanted yes or no answers to her battery of questions, but by then everything was a long story. I tried to convince her that this was a big mistake and begged her to let me call Dr. Mizner. She said I could call him, and as I dialed I felt certain that he would agree I didn't belong here. I reached his answering service, and when he buzzed me back, his voice was curt. I started crying, telling him what had happened in the park, blubbering that I had made a big mistake.

"What do you expect," he said, "when you go all over town telling people that you want to jump off a bridge?"

I was stunned.

"I think I made a mistake coming here."

"I can't help you now," he said.

Six

Shooting the Moon

Sunny von Bulow, it was rumored, was resting peacefully in an adjoining wing of the hospital I checked into that bitterly cold January day. It was said that she had a full-time staff of nurses and beauticians who provided makeup, coiffure, manicure, and pedicure every day of her comatose life. It seemed a sad irony that someone in a coma had her appearance more under control than I did.

In the days following my admission, there was much that I had to face. Not least of which was my weight. When the nurse weighed me, she did this slow dance up the scale a few pounds at a time, moving the balance to the right. For my whole life, every time I've been weighed, it seems to drag out this way. Some nurses have commented that I'm heavier than I appear, but this doesn't exactly make me feel better. Sometimes, just to get it over with, I blurt out my weight. This time I just stood there staring at the number: 176. *Oh, my god.* There was the fact that I had voluntarily signed myself in, and no longer had the right to sign myself out. I had arrived with nothing but my wallet and a poem—no clothes, no books, not even my address book. I had to deal with Mizner's anger, which I had felt radiating from the emergency room phone. And my poor parents—how could I face them? Still, I remained focused on my unwieldy body. The Joan Baez lady at the eating disorders unit had taken my food problem seriously. When I described the torture of failing again and again in OA, she had nodded emphatically.

"Your depression and your compulsive eating are inextricably linked," she said, weaving her fingers together the way we used to in playing "Here is the church, here are the people."

But there was something else as well. I felt relieved. Not that I wasn't scared; I had certainly done it this time.

Shooting the Moon

I had put myself in a place where I could no longer hide the terrible truth that I was a person who wanted to die, who courted death, whose breath was sour, whose skin smelled pasty.

I immediately wanted out and tried to persuade the nurses that I didn't belong here. But I also wanted in. Where else could I go? My childhood bedroom? The crawlspace beneath the stairs? Hadn't I eaten every corn chip and cupcake from every deli between 116th Street and the tip of Manhattan? There was nothing left to choke on. Where was I supposed to turn—another OA meeting, another qualification? One more sad story of a person destroying his life and building it back with the help of the goddamned Almighty? Was I really supposed to go back to Mizner's office and cry more wolf? There was that peak above the Hudson, the place that was shaping up to be my stairway to heaven until a messenger arrived, stepping out from behind a decidedly nonburning bush, in the form of a guy beating off. Not exactly *It's a Wonderful Life*.

I found comfort in the general sterility of the hospital room: the Dixie cup dispenser above the sink, the antibacterial soap, the venetian blinds. The ceiling was acoustic tile with tiny perforated dots in a pattern of circles. The windows didn't open. A red button above the light switch was marked EMERGENCY. I could feel the place happening around me, people moving in the hall, carts filled with foul-smelling hospital food rolling through. I was afraid to leave my room and investigate my surroundings, and no one bothered me.

A nurse explained that I wouldn't get to see the doctor assigned to my case until Monday, though a weekend doctor would drop by. That doctor turned out to be much nicer than the intake doctor, though she too clicked off a few notes on a clipboard. She asked if I had any questions and I didn't. Instead I stared at her beautiful brown leather boots and admired her thin legs inside them. I had always wanted legs like that.

My parents came the next day. They arrived with ashen faces, as if I had died. For a moment I saw how they would have looked if I had killed myself. They tried to look brave, tried to get comfortable in that unwelcoming room. They didn't ask what had happened, at least not directly. I figured they had talked to either Mizner or the weekend doctor. And I didn't know what to say.

After a while my mother took out a small pad of paper, and in her large luxurious script started making a list of things to bring me. I had always loved my mother's handwriting. In every other aspect of her life, she opted for plain, tailored, discreet. But the large loops of her script and the elaborate doodles she drew down the margins of the phone book pages filled me with hope that beneath her practical demeanor was a hidden love of extravagance.

"What do you need, honey?" she asked, her pen poised.

"Sweats," I said. I was dying to get out of my jeans. They had cut off my circulation weeks ago, but I was still pouring myself into them every day. Had anyone ever successfully killed themselves with their Calvin Kleins?

My mother stayed focused. "What else? Underwear? A toothbrush?"

"That's good." I could barely look at her. If only we were going over the contents of my camp trunk, if only she were sewing those little printed labels into my clothes again, her glasses sliding down her nose, the piles of socks and undershirts and underpants like a little city around her feet.

"Come on, what else?"

"A notebook," I said. "Spiral." I had kept diaries since I was eight years old. When I started college I switched to spiral notebooks, which I called journals.

"Good," she said, and wrote it down.

We decided we wouldn't decide anything about school just yet. We wouldn't tell anyone just yet. My mother would write a check for my roommate and drop it in the mail with a vague note. We would wait for the doctor. I would get some medication. Everything would be fine. *Everything would be fine.* My mother must have said it a thousand times.

My father talked about the traffic, the parking, the deli a few blocks up, the last remaining sign of what once had been a thriving Jewish neighborhood. We filled that first visit with small talk, though just beneath the surface chatter I kept asking myself how I had brought them here, to this.

My mother had always declared that everything was all or nothing for me, the criticism inherent in the observation. I never understood why extremes were to be avoided. Wasn't having passion a good thing? But what passions exactly had I been pursuing? Poetry? Thinness? And what of these pursuits over the last six months? What had I been doing but making a nest for myself of cellophane and wax wrappers, the detritus of a six-month binge that brought me to a perch from which I couldn't jump? Was this all, or was this nothing?

As they were getting ready to leave, my mother took

my hands in hers. Her nails, perfectly manicured and polished every day of her life, were slightly chipped. She had missed her Saturday-morning nail appointment on my account. I never exactly admired her perfect nails so much as relied on them as a barometer of her well-being. But now, when she took my hands, I saw her face register their horrible condition: my nails bitten down and bloody, maroon clots pooled in the corners.

"Poor little *hentelas,*" my mother said, rubbing my hands.

Tears burst from my eyes at my mother's sweet sympathy. Until then we had made every effort to shield each other from the fact that I was in a loony bin, that I had fallen apart, that I had been trying to kill myself.

My mother and father were fumbling with their coats and their parting words. They would be back on Monday, they would bring what I needed, my older sister sent her love. On hearing that, I wiped my eyes and asked if that was all she said. My sister and I had always been competitive, each of us the other's worst enemy. When I first went to see Dr. Parker at Yale, she had said that I just wanted attention; the comment still stung, in part because it was true.

"What else did she say?"

"Well, she's concerned, of course," my mother said, working the large buttons of her camel's-hair coat into their holes.

"How do you mean?"

"Concerned."

"About what exactly? Is she embarrassed?"

"No, it's not that, honey," my mother said, as if that weren't an issue on anyone's mind.

"Then what, I want to know." When I was little I was relentless in my pursuit of answers to the kinds of questions adults avoided. My parents often thought I'd become a lawyer.

"She's concerned she'll have to take care of you."

"What?" At first the meaning of her words didn't even register. "Take care of me? What are you talking about?"

"She's worried about after we're gone."

My mother was fifty-two, my father fifty-six. In a flash I saw my sister's version of the future: me at forty, fifty, sixty, pushing a grocery cart up Central Park West, wearing rags and talking to the pigeons. I was her nightmare vision of the mentally ill. Only worse: I would be her burden.

"What the fuck is she talking about?" I started screaming, convulsing with rage as this scenario played out in my mind. My sister pretending to worry about me, colluding with my parents and painting some tragic tableau, with her in the starring role as both hero and martyr in one brilliant stroke.

I screamed and cursed until a nurse rushed in to see if everything was all right. It wasn't. My parents fled. An orderly arrived with two white pills in a small paper cup, its pleats as neat as a Catholic girl's skirt. I was told they would help me calm down. I joked about a straitjacket, and they said I could have one if I wanted. I declined, although there was something tempting about losing it completely, becoming that woman my sister imagined. *Fuck her.* I cried until I fell asleep. I dreamed I was stuck in a tree. My father was in a cherry picker trying to save me, but he couldn't operate the gears to maneuver close enough.

∞

Dr. Rostenberg arrived Monday morning carrying the ubiquitous clipboard. He introduced himself and sat down in the visitor's chair, stretching his long legs out in front of him. I took in the gray slacks, socks, and loafers from my perch on the bed. I was surprised at how meek he looked. Behind the pale pink frames of his eyeglasses he looked like a tiny white mouse with pink eyes. In a nasal voice he read back some of my intake information: I had arrived Friday night, I had been referred by the eating disorders group at Columbia, I was a graduate student at Columbia. Yes, yes, yes. What did I study? All too aware how clichéd the stereotype was, I dared to say it: poetry. He asked me about Dr. Mizner and whether I had been on medication. He wasn't particularly interested in my weight, even said I might have to gain more before I got better. He suggested that the weight was a form of protection. That idea came to me as a revelation, though I rejected it almost instantaneously. Any cure that required me to gain more was part of the problem, not part of the solution.

Dr. Rostenberg was fixated on my inability to make eye contact. He asked why I couldn't look at him. When he wouldn't let it drop, I stared even harder at his shoes.

"Why do you suppose you can't look at me?"

I shrugged.

"Were you able to look at your other psychiatrist, Doctor"—he glanced down at the chart and pulled up the name—"Dr. Mizner?"

Dr. Mizner's red carpet appeared before my eyes. I remembered the way the fringe at the end bunched together and how I wanted to comb it like hair. I felt my face go hot. I shook my head as if to clear the image, but instead I started to cry again. I had cried more in two days at the hospital than I had for years. When I was little, my older sister had ruthlessly teased me for crying during an episode of *The Patty Duke Show*. From that day forward I vowed never to cry, and I rarely succumbed. I prided myself on sitting through the great Hollywood tearjerkers like *Love Story* and *Terms of Endearment* without producing a single tear. I stoically sat through the Broadway show *Bent* as grown men around me sobbed.

Years later I would find out that my mother didn't cry during the funeral service for my little sister. Instead, I was told, she broke her caps gritting her teeth. I was told she didn't go to the cemetery afterward. Sometimes I would imagine my mother visiting the grave, resting her back against the stone, shaking a Tareyton from its glossy white packet. My mother inhaled a cigarette as if each puff were her last, deeply and with every molecule of her being. She exhaled in equal measure, a small stream escaping from her nostrils to meet the stream of smoke from her lips. In my vision, she would sit there only as long as it took to smoke her cigarette. There would be no conversation with God, no prayers for the little girl. My mother didn't plan to meet anyone in heaven. She would just snuff out the cigarette, snap her purse, and survey the sky. She wouldn't assign any sad meaning to clouds nor feel encouraged by sunshine. She would get back in her car and drive off.

❧

"Do you think you could look at me?" Dr. Rostenberg's annoying nasal voice brought me back to the moment. I wanted Mizner back. I wanted to make things right with him. I glanced up at Rostenberg as if I were wearing bifocals, my head still down, my eyes rolling up.

"That's good," he said as if to a pet, and I glanced away.

"Betsy," he said, "I'd like you to stay here for a week or two so we can observe you, and I'd like to start you on an antidepressant immediately. Have you ever been on Tofranil?"

I faced him and said I hadn't.

"I'll check back in with you tomorrow. Oh, one more thing. It might help to get out of your room a little and mix with the others."

I realized then that I had been under observation all weekend. I hadn't been safe in my cocoon at all. The clipboard had been filling with details of my sleeping, eating, mixing or not mixing, along with my vitals.

Shooting the Moon

All new arrivals were put on constant observation until the staff decided they were no longer suicidal. Privileges were added incrementally. First you might be allowed off the floor with a fellow patient. Eventually you could go outside for a smoke, then you might get a half-day pass. A weekend pass usually signaled that you would soon be leaving the hospital for good.

Over the next few days, as I ventured out of my room, I began to learn the drill. Control of the couches and the channel changer was the domain of the patients who had done the most time and acted as if they owned the place, like college seniors. Newcomers, however, were always first to line up for meds; the cool people hung back. I was amused to see that even in the bin, the great losers' lounge of the soul, it was still important to hang back, be last in line. And in this way the ward was no different from any other institution I had ever belonged to since high school.

❧

When my mother returned with the familiar bag from Jimmy's Army Navy Store I felt a huge swell of relief. When I had first discovered Jimmy's at thirteen I believed I had found Mecca. Here were all the clothes I wanted to hide inside: army fatigues, BVD T-shirts, Lee jeans, which were decidedly more generous in the hips than Levi's. But inside the bag my mother brought, instead of the basic black or gray sweats I had asked for, were sweats in turquoise and cherry red. My relief turned to rage. Couldn't she just this once bring what I asked for? Did I have to "maximize my looks" for the other mental patients and the orderlies? Why now, when I was a captive on a locked ward of a loony bin, did my mother feel the need to reassert her ideas about color?

I should have been grateful that she came at all, that she brought me clothes. I knew I was a spoiled, ungrateful brat, but I no longer had any elasticity. When a food tray arrived with a Salisbury steak swimming in a vile-smelling brown sauce instead of the hamburger I expected, I wanted to throw the whole thing on the floor in a temper tantrum. I was barely managing to accept that I was among the stale-breathing, mildly-trembling chorus of mental patients shuffling in a meds line or watching *Who's the Boss?* on vinyl couches in a linoleum-tiled TV room. I was trying to hold it together. But when I saw those turquoise and cherry red sweats, I wanted to strangle someone.

The ongoing game of hearts on the ward was presided over by Kyle, a twenty-year-old from Fordham University. More than six feet tall, he had a long shag haircut with bangs, which he habitually brushed aside with an oddly delicate wave of his hand. He was a gentle giant type who presided over the other patients with physical domination and silent strength. No one had any idea why Kyle was on the floor. He seemed fine, if a little surly. He refused to eat the hospital food, so his parents or brothers brought him bags of McDonald's cheeseburgers, which he stashed in his room. He carried three or four burgers on his person at all times in the large side pockets of his fatigues. I would have loved a McDonald's burger, but I didn't dare ask my parents for any food. Still claiming that all I needed was abstinence, I tried to stick to the 1,200-calorie diet provided on the three daily hospital trays, though I often snagged an extra serving or two of Jell-O or vanilla pudding.

I was a big-time card player from a card-playing family. Once, playing gin rummy with my grandmother, she told me I'd rub the crack off the queen if I held it any longer. The vulgarity was over my head; how did she know I had the queen? I had played cards through summer camp and high school study halls, and I was desperate to get into the game. So I just hung around and smoked, waiting for my opportunity. And eventually, when one player or another was called away for a phone call or had a visitor, I got my chance to join the game. Kyle could see that I knew what to do with a hand, and soon we became regular partners. This elevated me considerably in the hierarchy.

We cemented a regular foursome that included Kyle and me as partners. Third at the table was Vin, a cocaine addict who played three-card monte with his urine specimens—he was always trying to find a new way to slip the nurses a clean specimen. Vin was a waiter/actor who wore muscle shirts to impress us with his biceps, each one magnificently tattooed with an eagle. He was brilliant at doing impressions, especially of greasers past, and was macho in every respect except the way he smoked, never truly inhaling. Our fourth was an elderly gentleman from Queens. Cy had one daughter whose visits seemed to irritate him. He had a full head of white hair, which he restlessly raked with a black comb. Though he was a mediocre card player, he was good for laughs. Cy, we discovered, was a recent widower who had made himself a Clorox cocktail one night before turning in for what he hoped would be eternity.

It was at the card table that I began to learn what

everyone was in for. I discovered which doctors were crazy themselves, which nurses were generous with the stool softener. It was where I learned how to fake a urine test, how to hide and stockpile meds, how to get more Jell-O. All we ever did was schtick, riffing about a nurse's fat ass, an orderly's drinking problem. Vin did impressions of the patients returning from electric shock therapy, gelling his hair out in points and walking into walls.

Two weeks into my stay, all the patients were herded into the day room and told that we would be on constant observation for the next twenty-four hours. We could not stay in our rooms or leave the ward. In smaller group sessions we were told that a new arrival had committed suicide. He had been on the floor only three hours. The staff was frantic, interrogating us in session after session about how this made us feel. No one was stating the obvious: we didn't know who he was—how upset were we supposed to get? But they kept after us. Finally, Lynn Burton, a social worker who ran a lot of the sessions, smacked her clipboard onto her lap.

"People," she said, "someone has killed himself on our floor. Doesn't anyone have anything to say?"

Billy, a kid who must have been one of the first Ritalin guinea pigs, started whistling and tried to sit in

Lynn's lap. When she pushed him away, he made an exaggerated sad face.

Kyle was tapping his foot, eyes on the ground.

"Does anyone worry about our ability to take care of you?" Lynn asked, her voice going softer, less aggressive.

"Not at all," said Cy. "You're doing a wonderful job. When can I go home?"

"Mr. Bloomberg, it would be more helpful if you could share your feelings about what happened on our ward."

"Oh, that's a shame, a terrible shame," said Cy, without a trace of irony.

Lynn told us that our rooms would be searched and that we'd have to stay in the day room except during therapy sessions. This was standard emergency procedure. The doctors and nurses made more huddles that day than a football team. There was great concern for copycat acts.

That night at the hearts game we talked about the mechanics of the thing. We had heard that the guy hanged himself from a doorknob with the belt from his terry-cloth robe. Was this even possible? We tried to imagine it. Vin slumped himself under a doorknob and held an imaginary noose over his head. And then, in our typically perverse fashion, we talked about other ways to kill oneself on the ward. It would take more than a little ingenuity, given that we were forbidden sharp objects, leather belts, and now fabric belts as well. We talked about breaking into the meds room, but figured they'd be able to pump our stomachs before any real damage was done. Vin said he could get a gun within a two-block radius of the hospital. Kyle said he'd seen a guy at Bellevue smash the TV and slash his wrists with the glass. I wondered if he was talking about himself.

"I'd pull a Cy," said Vin. "Dive for the cleaning cart and swig the ammonia." He cracked himself up with that.

Cy shot him a dirty look and played the wrong card.

"I'd swallow the mercury from a thermometer," Kyle proudly announced, simultaneously winning the suicide one-upmanship sweepstakes and shooting the moon.

Tofranil gave me heart flutters, so the doctors prescribed another medication. When that didn't work they wanted to try a type of antidepressant known as an MAO inhibitor. The only problem was that you had to stay away from certain foods absolutely, including cheese. Dr. Rostenberg thought I could handle it, but I was certain I would commit suicide with a large pizza. He didn't see my weight issue as life-threatening; he believed my eating disorder was a symptom of a deeper problem. They tried another medication in the Tofranil family, and my fluttering heart finally acclimated to the dose. I lied to Dr. Rostenberg and the staff and said I felt better, when I was just biding my time.

After I had been there a month, my privileges were bumped up and I was allowed a four-hour pass with visitors on the weekends, meaning I could go get a deli sandwich with my parents when they came. We became very fond of that deli in Washington Heights, with its briny sour pickles and fragrant rye bread. When I was given a full-day pass, we decided to go see a Broadway show. We traveled down to midtown and my father slipped into a tiny ticket broker's office while my mother and I waited in the double-parked car. We didn't say much, but all the excitement I used to feel when my father would disappear, only to reappear with fourth-row seats to *Mame* or *My Fair Lady* or *Godspell* or *Pippin,* was lost. I watched a homeless man pick through a garbage can. My father returned with tickets to see Whoopi Goldberg.

"What kind of a name is that?" my mother said.

"She's black," I said.

"Is she Jewish?"

"I don't know."

"What kind of a name is Whoopi?"

"It's a hot ticket," my father said, easing the car down the street in search of a parking garage. We ate lunch at Joe Allen's. Though desperate for the ribs, I ordered a salad. The bread basket had little corn muffins, which I couldn't resist.

We had second-row seats, and as we sat down I gazed up at the great dome of the theater, the brass railings, the chandeliers. The place filled with the chewy noisiness of a theater crowd, the smells of perfume, mink, and silk. I was suddenly overcome with self-consciousness; could people tell I was on a day pass from a loony bin? Was I really at a Broadway show with my parents? What were we trying to prove? Finally the lights came down. Whoopi Goldberg's characters cut right through me. Her monologues in the voices of junkies and homeless people were deeply political, the humor stitched with anger. The show made me feel that much more pathetic, indulged, unworthy. My own self-loathing was like a furnace: there was nothing that didn't feed it. Everything was consumed in the flame.

Besides my parents, I allowed only two people to visit. The first was Bettina from OA. I was still struggling in my head with the tenets of the program and had called her looking for forgiveness. Maybe I wanted to impress upon her that my problems were more serious than the program could address, hoping she would see fit to absolve me or at least forgive my weight gain.

I was resting when the nurse brought her to my room. I meant to get off my bed to greet her, but she seemed harried and stern at the same time, and I stayed put. She had brought white tulips and anxiously looked around for a place to put them.

"You can use that pitcher," I said and gestured toward the mauve plastic container on the tray. Bettina's translucent skin had an oily sheen. I watched as she removed her black wrap and set her bag down. I knew in a moment it had been a big mistake to have asked her up.

"Deena celebrated two years of abstinence," she said too brightly. "And Carl sends his love."

I nodded as if happy to hear the news.

"And I got a new job, finally. I'm managing a gallery in SoHo. Well, south of SoHo, but it's really cool."

I kept nodding. "That's great, that sounds really great."

She was smiling at her own good news. Then she pulled her chair in closer. "Tell me, do you really think you need to be here?" Her voice sounded softer now, almost conspiratorial. Bettina wanted some kind of explanation and I had none to offer. Mostly I was ashamed of my size. When had she seen me last? Thirty, forty, fifty pounds ago?

"Betsy, what happened?"

I didn't know how to answer. I was no longer sure which version was true. Had I tried to kill myself? Was I just trying to get attention? Pulling a Plath? There was nothing sexy or glamorous or dark or poetic about me. I was hardly creating the dark sonnets of my soul on the ward. Mostly I was watching TV, biding my time playing cards, and trying to get my paws on another serving of Jell-O.

"I don't know," I said weakly.

"What are they doing for you?"

"Well, they've been trying me on different medications." As I said it my mouth went dry.

"What kind of medications?"

"Antidepressants."

"That's a mistake," she said. "You need to get out of here. All you need is the program. And your Higher Power."

I felt the room go cold with her presence. She clasped her hands and leaned forward on the bed, resting her forehead on her hands, locked in prayer. I moved toward the wall, feeling like Linda Blair faced with the priest. She wanted to expunge the demon that had seized my soul. I had lived with the program for more than ten years—ten years of daily torture, of failure, of a tape loop that ran through my brain: feast or famine, binge or abstain, live or die. Whatever she thought of my being here, however much she needed to cling to the twelve steps, I couldn't believe that she had come to proselytize. To pray.

Fuck her and fuck the program.

When she left, I dumped the tulips in the garbage.

⌘

John tracked me down through my parents. He told my mother that he had been calling my Inwood apartment for months and wondered if I had changed the phone or if something was wrong. My mother relayed his message; she wanted to know what, if anything, she should tell him. We still weren't exactly telling people. My whereabouts was being treated as a national secret. I took his number, but I didn't call right away. Shame flooded in every time I thought about standing in line at the bank of pay phones. When I finally parked myself in the glass booth and pressed the numbers, I knew only one thing for certain: I would not allow him to see me. By the end of the conversation, I was giving him directions and visiting hours.

Shooting the Moon

When John arrived, I spotted him before he saw me. He was attempting a certain nonchalance amid the clatter of carts and fluorescent lights and looked the other way when a patient gave him a big loony smile. I imagine he was anxious about seeing me, about what he would find, whereas all I could think of was my weight. The last time he had seen me I was fifty pounds lighter. That I was depressed and suicidal didn't seem nearly as mortifying.

Just as John caught my eye, the head nurse, Wendy, caught him by the elbow and took him inside the nurses' station. Through the meds window I could see that she was explaining something to him. She was emphatic, chopping at the air with her free hand. I could tell he was listening intently, nodding his head to show that he understood. As they wrapped up, she looked at the face of her enormous wristwatch and marked the time on her clipboard.

John came toward me, and tears came to my eyes. He put his arm around me, sideways, buddylike, and pulled me to him. Before I could say anything he told me he was allowed to take me out for two hours. I grabbed my coat and we fled the hospital like two teenagers.

"What was Wendy telling you?" I asked as we disappeared into the foot traffic of upper Broadway.

"She was just giving me the rules—no drugs, no drinking, that kind of thing."

"And?"

"And what?"

"What else did she say?"

"You really want to know?"

"Come on."

"She told me you had been suicidal, that I couldn't let you out of my sight."

"Great."

"Is it true?"

"I don't know."

"Should I be scared?"

I could tell John had taken the nurse's warning with all the seriousness of the altar boy he once was. If I were a chalice, he would have held me with his two small Catholic hands tightly cupped so as not to spill a drop.

"Well, should I?"

A perverse part of me wanted to fake a quick getaway just then or jump in front of the oncoming traffic.

We went to the Cloisters and walked and talked and smoked. It was one of those surprisingly windless winter days when you can feel the sun through a thin layer of cloud cover, when the smoke from your cigarette looks like steam from an engine. I saw my little espaliered pear tree and gave her a nod. *Still here.* I wondered if my mother could have directed my growth, the way someone had trained the branches of the pear tree. Hadn't I had a strong will ever since I was little? I thought of Dr. Parker and his prediction all those years ago that I would end up in a hospital if I didn't take lithium. Was I fulfilling his prophecy or my own?

~

"Poets are supreme egoists," John said, not exactly an insult.

I laughed and lit another cigarette. I wanted to tell him that I loved him. But I just stared into the distance.

"I've thought about you every day, you know."

At this, tears again. Quick, out of the corner.

"I was kind of shocked," he continued.

"Then?"

"Pissed."

"And now?"

John sat quietly for a while. I could tell that he was choosing his words with great care.

"Everyone wonders," he started.

"About killing themselves?"

"How close they come."

I told him I was sorry to disappoint him. "I disappointed myself."

John looked at the ground. His face tightened.

Then we really looked at each other. I remembered that day at Playland six months earlier, when we lay on the beach and the day stretched into an endless dream. The girl in that swimsuit and the girl in her sweatsuit. I was untouchable then, untouchable now.

A week before my release date, Kyle, Vin, Cy, and I sat down to a game of hearts. We were all more irritable than usual, and Vin immediately started picking on Cy. Later, when Cy made a mistake that cost Vin his chance to shoot the moon, Vin jumped on him.

"How many brain cells?" he said, nudging Cy with his elbow.

"What are you talking?" Cy said, slowly collecting his cards.

"The cocktail. The bleach. How many brain cells you fry?"

"Leave him alone," Kyle said dully from behind his hand.

"Let him answer. I'd like to know what kind of a handicap we have going over here."

Cy drooped in his seat. You could tell that as a child he had been easily defeated, often picked on. And even now, late in life, after the trauma of losing his wife and a botched suicide attempt, he still invited antagonism, especially from guys like Vin, classic bullies.

"He's old," Kyle said, hoping to end Vin's aggression, appeal to his better angel.

"Shut your face, Dough Boy." Vin flexed his arm muscle. He was a cock, all swagger and primping, but he could be mean, too. Kyle was kind of pasty and chubby, but you didn't want to provoke him.

"Boys," Cy cried. "Let's play the game."

"I can't play with you." Vin slapped the newly gathered deck out of Cy's hands and sent the cards flying.

"Come on," I said, "he made one mistake. Let it go." I had already scooped up half the deck.

As Vin got up, his chair fell backward. He kicked it away and sank down in a chair in front of the TV. *The Odd Couple* was on. I asked Cy if he was okay, and he just shook his head before excusing himself. He walked off down the hallway, his head hanging low, then swatted the air with his right arm in a gesture I had seen my grandfather do a million times when he heard or ate something he found disagreeable: *Feh!*

I shuffled the deck and dealt out a hand for gin. Sitting there alone with Kyle, with nothing left to lose, I finally asked him, point-blank, why he was there. I was prepared for him to dodge the question, to maintain the big mystery at the heart of the ward, but he answered.

"Tried to kill myself."

"How?"

"Which time?"

"Which time?"

"This is strike number three. I'm out." He laughed, amused by his own joke.

"Jesus. How'd you do it?"

"Pills."

"Wow." Not what I would have guessed. I had read somewhere that most women use pills and most men use guns. I had also read that most men succeed and most women do not. Kyle stretched out a leg and reached deep into the side pocket of his fatigues. He withdrew two cheeseburgers wrapped in yellow paper.

"Want one?"

Kyle had never offered anyone a burger from his personal stash as far as I knew. I declined, though I could have eaten seven.

"How'd you try before?"

Kyle hiked up his sleeve and showed me the inside of his wrist.

"Why did you want to kill yourself?"

"Dunno." He shrugged and unwrapped his cheese-burger, then tossed the balled-up wrapper overhead and made a rim shot into the garbage.

"Kyle, can I ask you something?"

"Yeah."

"How many pills does it take to overdose?"

"I dunno," he said. "I didn't exactly succeed."

"Ballpark."

My parents, doctors, and social workers had arranged for my outpatient therapy. For five days a week from nine to five I was to go to a day program for people with eating disorders and depression. Therapy was going to be my day job. *Hi, honey, I'm home.* I told Rostenberg and the team that I would be happy to go, though the idea of sitting around with a bunch of anorectics filled me with anxiety. Idiotic as it was, I was jealous of those women. Why didn't I have the requisite vanity or insanity to puke my guts up or just starve myself? I didn't believe that any amount of therapy would change me. Plus the program cost a small fortune and was not covered by insurance.

I was still smarting from a remark my mother had made early on to Dr. Rostenberg.

"What do people do who can't afford this kind of help?" she asked, her voice thick with resentment.

"They suffer, Mrs. Lerner," he said.

My social worker, Linda Peres, had also taken my side in family therapy. In one session my parents had infuriated her by suggesting that I was making up or self-willing my depression.

"Bullshit," she snapped. Later she told me that she wouldn't stand for that kind of insensitivity. When my father regaled her with stories of my early success, she interrupted him.

"Mr. Lerner, where are we now?"

He wasn't sure what she was getting at and didn't answer.

"Mr. Lerner, take a look at your daughter. Do you see where she is?"

He looked at her with an open question on his face.

"She's in a mental institution, Mr. Lerner. Do you know how she got here?"

Again my father was silenced.

"She wanted to kill herself. She's clinically depressed, and she has an eating disorder that I believe you are aware of. Am I right?"

My father nodded his assent.

"So, Mr. Lerner, can you stop telling stories about

when Betsy was fine and how wonderful your other daughters are. It's not helpful to Betsy."

I felt both protected by Ms. Peres and shamed for the way she had chastised my father. For all of Dr. Rostenberg's and Ms. Peres's support, I wanted what my parents wanted: to snap out of it, to get on with it. Sometimes I truly believed I was making everything up, had driven myself to that ledge. I wanted desperately to believe Dr. Mizner's version of my life—that I could stop the bingeing and the depression and the self-loathing as easily as turning off a spigot. It was my decision. Wasn't I just acting out? Couldn't I stop if I really wanted to?

In arranging the last piece of my posthospital care, the question of individual therapy came up. Dr. Rostenberg was willing to take me on but felt I had some unfinished business with Dr. Mizner, so he gave me a four-hour pass to arrange a session with Mizner and see if I might continue there. I was terrified that I would binge all the way there and all the way back, and I pretty much did.

At Mizner's building I gave Bob the Doorman an insanely friendly greeting, as if he were a long-lost friend. I was comforted to see that *schmutziga* piece of tape still holding his glasses together. I was barely seated in the waiting room when Mizner came out to greet me. In his office I took my seat but kept my pea jacket on. (Symbolic or just hiding the weight gain?) Then, for the first time in the nearly three years of our sessions, I pulled out a cigarette and lit it, dropping the match in the orange ashtray. After a few defiant puffs I started strong, told him about Rostenberg and the social worker and how they believed I suffered from a clinical depression that needed medicating and that I probably should have been med-icated months ago. I told him I was on an antidepressant. He just sat there, holding his unlit pipe. Maybe it was his lack of reaction, but I started to buckle. I began to apolo-gize to him for telling the other doctors that I was suici-dal when I didn't even know if I was. I apologized for not listening to him. When I finally stopped apologizing, he leaned forward in his chair, planted his elbows on his knees.

"Why don't you come on over to this side," he said.

For a moment I thought I had detected some kind-ness, thought that if I could just take the two steps across the carpet between us Mizner might console me. But then he finished the thought.

"Why don't you come on over to this side," he said, "and join the human race."

As he said those words it was as if the red carpet between us became the parted seas of biblical time. I was still desperate to please him, even as he rubbed me out, consigned me to the half-life I half-believed I deserved. I just sat there. When he asked me what I wanted to do, meaning continue with him or not, I made no move to answer. Mizner's body language told me he was becoming impatient. Finally, he looked at his watch and said, "Why don't you call me when your thoughts crystallize."

My thoughts crystallize? I had been sitting in front of him session after session, blowing up and slimming down while I suffered from crippling depressions. I had shared every last detail of my hideous sex life at his urging, all my fantasies. I had described every humiliating incident suffered at the hands of men and thoughtless friends. I had told him from the beginning, when he asked if I wanted to win, that I just wanted to cope. And he couldn't even help me do that. The therapy was all on his terms, though in truth my own terms were more terrible, for they were nonnegotiable: I was defined by my weight—end of conversation.

Every day I awoke inside a prison of my own making, my mind and body no longer serving to house a life but rather a life sentence. Mizner used to say that I was the judge and the hangman—but what of the person at the end of the rope? Had Mizner ever seen me hanging there by a thread? Now it became very clear to me: I would never return to his office. The room filled with the silence of his unanswered question. And then I heard the soft warble of my pigeon friends budging each other out on the ledge. I would leave the hospital. I would stockpile my antidepressants. I would swallow enough to kill myself.

My thoughts had crystallized.

Seven

Everybody Knows
This Is Nowhere

Wendy, the head nurse, walked by and gave me a tight smile. "Up early," she said, half question, half comment.

"Big day," I answered.

"Oh, that's right," she said, and turned the corner to unlock the meds room. Her forgetfulness or aloofness was uncharacteristic. Wendy was the most empathic and involved of the nursing staff, and I couldn't believe she had forgotten that it was my last day. I listened to her set up the meds, placing the little Dixies on the medication slips, opening the jars of pills and shaking them out like so much candy. I wondered how many pills they were going to trust me with for my first prescription. Should I hide this morning's dose under my tongue to get a start? How long would it take to have enough?

Waiting felt like all those last days of summer camp, when we would be sitting on a hill amid our trunks and duffels, signing address books and taking pictures. As the first cars started to roll in, signaling the arrival of the parents and the end of summer, I would watch the other girls break down in loud sobs as they recognized their parents' car. Sometimes a girl would scream and run away from her parents, making a swift trail through the littered baggage like a deer up a craggy hillside. I would usually cry, too, but not out of sadness for leaving a particular friend or for the passing of another summer. I just never knew how to say goodbye, though I desperately wanted to join the chorus of crying girls. Plus I dreaded getting into my parents' claustrophobic car, the smell of my mother's lipstick everywhere.

It seemed the same now, as I awaited my mother's arrival. I didn't know how to say goodbye to Kyle or Vin or even the old Clorox-swigger, whom I had come to feel great affection for. Over the weeks I had observed Cy go from being in complete denial about his suicide attempt to grappling with mourning the loss of his wife and his subsequent depression. I had watched as he and his daughter, who regularly participated in the family therapy sessions, took some steps toward reconciliation. I had the sense that he would be all right, that he would move in with his daughter, that they would make it work.

Hundred-to-one odds that Vin would use drugs the moment he was released. I had no idea about Kyle. He was still inscrutable to me and to the staff. He didn't seem to want to die, but that was all you could say for him. When he finally told me about his own attempts, his tone was as casual as if he were actually talking about the first three times he got up to bat.

I grew anxious as nine o'clock drew near. My mother arrived a little early, and we sat together quietly on the couch. She had come in with her face set for progress, for making a new start, but the longer we were kept waiting, the more her expression deflated. Each time she came to visit I saw strange weather pass over her face that I couldn't predict—clouds of anger, disappointment, resentment, despair. I had always been able to make everyone laugh, to win my mother with my precocious verbal skills and quickness. I still remember how delighted she was when I remarked that the cornfield near our house after a light snowfall looked like a man's beard stubble.

"That's a simile," she told me. "When you make a comparison using 'like' or 'as.'"

I wasn't sure what she was talking about.

"A simile," she repeated. "You said the field was like a man's beard. It's a perfect comparison. That's a simile." I could tell she had been delighted by my observation, and I looked everywhere to make more similes for her. Only now nothing about me was quick, fast, or bright. But when had it ever been perfect? Often my performances ended in tears, with my mother intoning that I didn't know when to stop, that I always had to push things. Many years later, when I was shoving food into my face on a wild binge or finding myself in the arms of a dangerous stranger in the East Village, I would hear my mother's incantation: *You don't know when to stop, you just don't know when to quit.* I wondered if she could read my mind now. How badly I wanted to be stopped.

Rostenberg came out of the nurses' station and told my mother that he'd like to speak with her privately.

"You," he said, "can wait right there." His voice was stern, and I began to panic as another twenty minutes went by and the morning therapy groups let out. The waiting area filled with patients lighting up between sessions. Some asked why I was still hanging around, joked that I couldn't get enough of the place. Kyle was nowhere to be seen. Wendy also had been avoiding me. Finally, my mother returned with Rostenberg, her face grim. She didn't look at me. Rostenberg ushered me into one of the small offices. The room, completely white, held a table, two chairs, no windows. I felt giddy.

"So, you want to tell me what's going on?" Rostenberg clasped his hands in front of him.

"You want to tell me."

"I'm not fooling around here, Betsy."

I sat there thinking about my mother parked outside on the wooden bench. About the view of the George Washington Bridge from my room, how it looked more like a postcard than the thing itself.

"I don't know what you want to hear," I finally said.

"Well, I'd like to know about a certain card game, for starters."

Kyle had ratted me out. I couldn't believe it. Stunned, I tried to play dumb a little longer.

"What about it?"

"I'm not playing games here, Betsy. You're not going anywhere, so you might as well admit what you've got on your mind."

food and loathing

"What do you mean I'm not going anywhere? I'm packed. I'm leaving today." My voice was half-pleading, half-incensed.

"Look, your friend Kyle told Wendy that you wanted to know how much medication you'd need to take to kill yourself."

"We always talk about shit like that. He said he was going to swallow the mercury from the thermometer."

"You're on C.O."

"I cannot believe you would take his word over mine. Don't you think it's just possible that he was calling out for help himself?" This angle actually seemed plausible to me.

"No. I think he did a very difficult thing that was against his own code of friendship because he has grown to care about you."

"He doesn't care about anyone or anything except his cheeseburgers. The guy is a sociopath and you know it."

"Here's what I know: you're not going anywhere and you're on constant observation until you come clean with us. Would you like to say goodbye to your mother?"

I knew I should say goodbye, but I couldn't face my mother. I couldn't face anyone: not Kyle, not Wendy. Not my fucking fuckhead self. I was so completely ashamed that I had given myself away by asking Kyle about lethal doses. How could I do this to my mother? It wasn't fair. She always said life wasn't fair, meaning don't have any expectations. But a mother expects her children will outlive her. She had already lost one daughter to pneumonia, to water overwhelming the lungs of a little girl. Now she had to face another: only it wasn't the water choosing me; I was choosing the water.

I sat in my room all day until bedtime. An orderly named Rufus sat outside and sneaked me a few cigarettes (we were allowed to smoke only in the common areas). Mostly I sat with my back to the door and stared straight ahead at the porous white cement wall.

"Mind if I eat this?" Rufus asked when I refused my lunch tray.

"Nope."

"Care for a smoke?" he'd ask and shake his package of Camels at me. "Why's a pretty girl like you so miserable?"

No answer.

"I have a daughter your age."

I remained silent.

"She just had a little girl. That makes me a grandfather. Can you guess how old I am?"

I didn't guess.

"I'm forty-two. You don't believe me." Rufus went on this way as if I were participating in the conversation. He didn't need me to guess or answer or *ooh* or *aah,* not even when he took out the picture of the little baby, with its smooshed-in face and lacy white bonnet. I wanted to rip the picture in half. Instead, I returned to the seat where I had been keeping vigil.

Eventually I came out. It was night, the halls were quiet. I heard the canned laughter of *The Tonight Show* as I made my way down to the TV room. Rufus was shadowing me, as ordered. Kyle was at the card table, playing solitaire. I sat on one of the couches facing the TV and took out a cigarette. Rufus was right behind me with a lighter. I studiously avoided eye contact with Kyle. I heard the unmistakable sounds of his unwrapping a burger, tossing the wrapper, and missing. He lumbered toward the garbage can to retrieve the yellow paper. As he leaned over to pick it up, he looked at me from beneath his bangs, his face hopeful for a sign of my forgiveness.

I was ready for my close-up. Rostenberg had arranged an intake interview for me with the staff of New York State Psychiatric. Since I couldn't attend the day program, they had to find alternative care, and New York State, the teaching arm of Columbia Presbyterian, was a long-term facility, and free. Naturally there was a catch or, in this case, two: first, my parents had to be willing to attend family and multifamily therapy sessions, and second, I had to be willing to work with a second-year resident as my therapist. My grief-stricken parents were willing to do anything at that point, and I didn't think the resident would be a problem. Still, there was this little detail of the interview and getting in.

I was ushered into a dingy room occupied by dingy people—five women and one man. The women all wore some variety of calf-length skirt, fuzzy multicolored sweater, enormous beads, and shapeless hair. The director, Dr. More, was all head. He wore a dove-gray silk vest buttoned from top to bottom. He had an annoying way of elongating his vowels. I felt better picking out their imperfections.

"Tell us about yourself," Dr. More began.

I started with Columbia, then went back to age fifteen and my first big weight loss in OA. I highlighted the critical times: Dr. Parker and the lithium, graduation, the abortion. I talked about Dr. Mizner and how Dr. Rostenberg had helped me get free of that situation. The women sat expressionless. Dr. More pulled his feet in under his chair and placed his hands on his thighs. For a moment I thought we were going to play pat-a-cake. Then I told them about the last few weeks at the hospital, my guilt over my parents, my own confusion about my problems. I told them about the bridge, how I both wanted to jump and didn't want to, how I was grateful for the guy beating off in the woods and grateful for Kyle. I told them how I might just be crying wolf because I wasn't turning out to be the person I thought I would be.

Finally, Dr. More cocked his head, and the five women turned in unison to watch him deliver his judgment. The room became quiet and I became more apprehensive, completely uncertain of their impressions of me and my pathetic monologue.

"I have just one question for you." Dr. More leaned forward. "What is it that you're withholding from us now?"

"That I want you to take me," I said, my eyes filling fast, "to help me."

He smiled and nodded. "We will."

When I returned to the unit, Dr. Rostenberg was waiting for me. For some reason I didn't want to tell him that I had gotten in. I wanted him to suffer a little. After all, he was handing me over—I wouldn't be his problem anymore. Why should he get off so easy?

"Well?" he said, leaning into his clipboard. I was familiar with this stance by now. They all did it, as if we were unruly children who tested the limits of patience. I imagined him for a moment in swim trunks with clipboard and whistle, his nose greased up in white emollients to keep it from burning. I saw his skinny legs and rib cage, a peek of brown bushy hair from his armpits, which vaguely unnerved me. I was lost in my fantasy, as often happened to me on the floor. I'd have an overwhelmingly powerful vision of a nurse or patient in an alternate reality. Once I imagined Nurse Wendy eating out a lover on a plaid picnic blanket. And then I could never get the picture out of my head.

"How did it go?" Rostenberg asked, trying to sound upbeat.

"How did it go?"

"Did you get in?"

"Did I get in?" I wasn't sure how long I could keep up vaguely mocking him. I wanted to cry. He had been the one who took me seriously, and I hated him for it. I realized then that the interview was probably just a formality and he already knew the answer. Most likely I had been set up. I was sick to think of how I had blubbered and carried on in there, even though I had finally told the truth, finally asked for help.

Rostenberg looked at me. His look said he didn't deserve what I was dishing out. His look told me that he had had enough, a concept I seemed incapable of grasping.

"Did you get in?" he asked again, his voice more controlled than I would have hoped. I hadn't gotten to him.

"I got in." There, I'd said it. I'm going off to the big house, hurrah for me.

"How does it feel?" Rostenberg was still earnest, even in the face of all my obnoxious behavior.

"Well, it's not exactly Harvard."

Once the decision was made, I felt a flood of fury toward my parents. I sensed they were not happy with this turn of events, would rather have spent every nickel of their savings to keep me from being locked up in another loony bin. I saw in New York State Psychiatric a chance for real independence. If my parents paid for my treatment, I reasoned, I would never get well. The consequences of choosing a state institution, however, did not fail to escape me. I packed and repacked my suitcase. I flossed my teeth until my gums bled.

I had told no one in my group where I was going.

"How do you feel about leaving tomorrow?" prompted the social worker, Lynn Burton, at the morning group therapy. Kyle, Vin, and the others turned to me, eager to hear my confession. I couldn't look at them. All our talk around the card table, at meals, and on the meds line was about getting out. How much we craved and missed our freedom. How fucked up it was to be here, on a locked ward, with the genuine psychos. We mocked everything: the doctors, the nurses, even our beloved Wendy, who I sometimes imagined as the big sister in *Peter Pan,* able to set us Lost Boys free on the wings of our meds.

Vin fashioned his fist into an imaginary mike and repeated the question in his best anchor voice. "So, tell us, Betsy, what exactly are your plans?" Then he stuck the mike in my face.

Everyone kind of laughed, and I choked back a tidal

wave rising up in my throat. Their attention was momentarily diverted when Wendy, joining us late, pulled up a chair. Lynn filled her in: "We were just asking Betsy how she felt about her plans." I hated the way all the therapists used that gentle kindergarten voice to state the obvious. Then Wendy nodded her knowing nod, which I also sort of hated. I wanted to say: *Wipe that phony empathic look off your face!* I wondered how much I really cared about any of these people. Coincidence had brought us together, nothing more.

"I'm going to another hospital," I finally said.

Vin did an exaggerated double-take, craning his neck and head in my direction. "Okay, then."

Kyle looked down, complicit, guilty.

"How do you feel about leaving?" Lynn asked.

"I don't know," was all I could manage.

"I think Betsy's doing a very brave thing," Wendy said. "For some reason this particular group, more than any I've seen, loves to make fun of the help afforded you here, but I think Betsy has added a lot to our groups, and she is taking a brave step to seek more help."

Then a very quiet girl whose name I could never remember, who wore a powder-blue sweatshirt appliquéd with a glittery angel, said in her quiet baby voice that she would miss me; I wanted to scalp her for the sentiment.

"Do you have any thoughts you'd like to share about where you're going?" Lynn was nothing if not a facilitator.

"Where the fuck are you going?" This from Vin, whose tone of voice implied that I had betrayed him with my silence on the subject.

"I'm going next door."

"What the fuck is next door?"

I couldn't say it. Every time I heard the name New York State Psychiatric I conjured an Edward Gorey drawing of a dungeon with a depraved man picking bugs off his scalp and popping them into his mouth.

~❦~

I spent the rest of the day trying to formulate something to say to Wendy and to Kyle. Wendy made it easy, giving me a big hug as she finished her shift, grasping my shoulders and looking me directly in the eye.

"You're gonna do great, you know."

My eyes filled in response.

"And that fellow, the one who came to visit."

I refocused my gaze as if to listen more carefully.

"He loves you, you know."

The tears came down in fast tracks.

Wendy hugged me again even harder. The zipper on her down vest dug into my cheek.

food and loathing

That night Kyle and I were the last ones sitting in the TV room. The musical guest on Carson had finished, and we knew it would be only a few minutes before we would be chased out. I was desperate to say something to him, to thank him, but I stayed silent, staring at his enormous sneakers, white leather Pumas with extra-thick laces threaded across like rungs on a ladder. His foot was dancing up and down in a crazy staccato. I wondered if he, too, felt some nervous energy between us, but thought better of it: the tremors were surely a side effect of his medication. I briefly wished that the couch was a car seat and that he was conspiring to put his arm around me, even though I wasn't really attracted to him. I imagined Kyle hairless and doughy beneath his Rangers hockey jersey, the smell of cheeseburgers always vaguely clinging. But I still wanted to draw near, to let him know that he meant something to me.

"Why don't you lovebirds say good night?" Rufus called.

I wanted to kill Rufus then, but he was just calling it like he saw it, as he always did. I had barely spoken Kyle's name when he closed his eyes and nodded, as if he already knew what I would say. I would never see him again. And I always wondered if someone, in turn, saved him.

∽

Rufus was assigned to take me over to my new digs. We walked through an elaborate series of tunnels that ran like a subway beneath the two hospitals. Rufus chattered as we walked, giving me the history of the tunnels, the weather report from Albany to North Carolina. He whistled a bit and commented no fewer than three times that I didn't seem crazy, each time circling his ear with his index finger. When the elevator opened onto my new ward, Rufus stepped sideways to hold the stainless steel door for me. "Madame, your castle," he said with a flourish. Then he let out a hearty laugh and squeezed both my hands in his. "Miss, you're gonna do just fine. You can trust Rufus on that."

No one came to greet me. The place, dimly lit, was quiet but for the far-off sounds of a TV in another room. As I walked further, I saw the lit window of the nurses' station. Inside, a tall woman with smooth olive skin and closely cropped hair was stepping around with rapid, jerky movements. I tapped on the glass, but she kept on in her busy fashion. I tapped again with a little more gusto.

"Not now, Susan, it's not time yet," she called out without looking up.

I didn't want to tap again so I just stood there. The place was unspeakably grim. Everything was made of cinder block, plastic, or linoleum. Every surface was dulled with grime. Some of the overhead fluorescent lights flickered. From the far end of the hall, a heavy girl in a chenille bathrobe was weaving her way toward the window. Her hair hung down in slabs on either side of her head. She knocked on the glass. At this third knock, the nurse whipped around and launched into a speech about taking meds with everyone else. I would soon discover that this was Susan's routine, hassling the nurses every day to get her pills before anyone else. In the middle of chastising Susan, the nurse noticed me and stopped mid-screed. "You must be Betsy. Have you been waiting long?"

I told her I had just been dropped off.

"I'm Sylvie," she said, coming around the station and extending her hand. I liked her right away. She wore jeans and black leather Reeboks. Her identification card dangled from a long necklace made of beautifully colored tiny glass beads. Most of all I loved her teeth—beautiful white tiles, the incisors resting a smidge forward, giving her smile a broad outline. I felt I could trust her. She raced back inside the nurses' station, apologizing all the while, preparing for what I would learn was noon feeding: meds and meal trays promptly dispensed at twelve for all those who couldn't leave the floor. Newcomers had no privileges until fully evaluated.

Sylvie soon had me filling out a sheaf of forms on a clipboard, which I dutifully attended to, perhaps too dutifully, as the other patients emerged from various treatment rooms and got in line for their meds. I could see that once again there was a hierarchy and that the hipper patients hung back. At the very end of the line were two women friends. One was a dark-haired beauty who carried herself through her hips, leaning into a stance of perfectly captured apathy. The other was a redhead in jeans and a black leather vest. A two-inch-wide studded leather bracelet encircled her left wrist, an oversize comb sprouted from her back pocket. The dark-haired one eyed me. The redhead was too busy bopping around, as if she were figuring out the chords to a song in her head.

Once everyone was squared away, Sylvie took me down a long, quiet hall to the dormitory. When we turned the corner, I saw a long corridor with beds on either side. I hadn't realized that I would no longer have a private room. It reminded me of the infirmary at camp, only there were no screened windows with the sweet smells of trees and sounds of summer wafting through. There were no windows at all. However oppressive the main room, the dormitory was far gloomier. I immediately spotted my assigned bed and cubby. All the others were marked by personal effects: a teddy bear here, an afghan there. Shoes lined up under a bed. Get-well cards taped to the headboard.

Sylvie put her arm around me and we walked over to my bed.

"I'm afraid I've got to go through your things and make an inventory," she said, clicking her Bic. I sat on the bed listening to her check off the sweatpants, sweatshirts, nightgown, and notebook. My toiletries were fine, she said. I'd have to ask for a safety shaver at the nurses' station. She went through some basic policies: wake up, lights out, showers, no smoking in the dormitory, prompt line-up for meds. We were responsible for getting to our therapy sessions on time. Community meeting once a week on Wednesday mornings—not to be missed. And privileges. The weekly tote board with each patient's name and privilege status. I was no longer on constant observation, but I had to stay on the floor and in the public rooms until further evaluation.

Everybody Knows This Is Nowhere

I had an appointment with my doctor at three o'clock, Sylvie told me. I was to make myself comfortable until then. My suitcase had to go into storage. I watched as Sylvie carried it away, one of the garment ties sadly trailing behind.

I stayed in the day room watching mindless daytime TV. A couple of patients roamed in and out. One girl's blue eyes appeared to be occluded with a white film. She lifted her head to the television as if to listen, then abruptly left. A preppie-looking fellow in jeans and a faded yellow Lacoste shirt walked in, pulled off his head-phones when he noticed me, and introduced himself as Danny. I asked him what he was listening to, as if we were dorm mates at college rather than hospital patients.

"Neil Young," he answered.

"I love Neil Young. Which album?"

"Everybody Knows This Is Nowhere."

I laughed in recognition, hearing the sad song in my mind, seeing the backyards where I played Frisbee, stoned out of my mind on a summer day, my friends around a keg, the music blaring through living room speakers, all of us convinced that the suburbs of New Haven were Nowhere, too. I fished out a pack of Marlboros from my jacket and offered one to Danny.

"Those things can kill you," he said, putting his

headphones back on and drifting toward the back of the room. At ten to three a woman in khakis and an untucked man's white dress shirt sat down next to me and opened a yogurt. She had sad blue eyes and elegant fingers. I admired the way she stirred the yogurt, slowly and with some pleasure. She put her feet up on the coffee table and smiled at me.

"Amy," she said and took a spoonful of the bluish yogurt.

"Betsy," I said.

"New?"

"First day."

"It'll get worse," she said, and smiled.

"Thanks." I looked at the clock.

"You have a three?" she asked.

"Yeah."

"Who with?"

"I don't know."

At that a young doctor wearing rimless glasses came into the day room, a clipboard by his side. He looked around the room as if lost, or maybe it was his glasses, at least half an inch thick.

"Oh, Jesus, you've got Junior."

I looked at the man again and was startled at his youthful appearance. Did he even shave?

Everybody Knows This Is Nowhere

"I'm Dr. Benedict," he said. "Are you Betsy?"

I said yes and we shook hands. He pointed toward the door and I followed him through, turning once to see what Amy was doing. She waved her spoon at me in a little circle of whoop-di-do and rolled her eyes. Dr. Benedict escorted me to another floor, down two corridors, and finally into the little room where we would meet three times a week for the duration of my stay. The room had two chairs, a desk, and no personal effects. Through the single window I could see another wing of the building. There was no ledge to speak of; I wouldn't be making friends with any pigeons here.

Dr. Benedict started with a battery of questions and studiously wrote down all my answers. I don't know which of us seemed more nervous. He was young enough to be my husband, I thought, noting the thick gold band on his ring finger. When we were closing in on fifty minutes, I asked him if he thought there was any hope for me. He smiled an awkward smile and sucked on the end of his pen.

"What do I need to do? Just tell me what to do." I was almost begging, exhausted from repeating my story, which now seemed to be just that: my story. Not necessarily the truth, not necessarily even remotely related to me. Just this story that began with the events of January

26 and ended here. Did any of it make a damn bit of difference? Wasn't it finally just a kid with a yen for cheeseburgers who had actually saved my life? Why should I think that any of these trained professionals could help me, least of all Junior?

"What do I have to do to get better?" I asked him again, this time nearly crying with frustration. *What do I have to do?*

"Show up and give it your heart and soul," he said, trying to sound convincing.

Right, I thought, a sardonic smile creeping across my face.

"You seem leery." Dr. Benedict cocked his head.

"So do you," I said.

❦

The hive of nocturnal activity in the dormitory was unsettling in the extreme that first night. Susan, the girl who loved her meds, snored like an old man. The girl with strange blue eyes had some sort of obsessive-compulsive disorder and kept making and unmaking her bed, folding and unfolding the clothes in her cubby. Across from me an anorectic was doing leg exercises under her covers and counting quietly. The whispering was worse than if she had just counted aloud. I tossed in my bed, trying to filter out the white noise of compulsion and sickness and loss. Everyone was desperate for something. I remembered being eight years old and wrapping myself in Ace bandages, trying to shock my parents into thinking I was the victim of some terrible accident. Down the way I heard someone softly sobbing. All sounds stopped when the night nurse on checks made her rounds. And then, as soon as she left, the sad cacophony started up again.

Eight

Watch Out Birds!

He was never "Junior" to me. I made a point of call-ing Dr. Benedict by his proper name. If someone asked me how things were going with Junior, I'd respond that I liked Dr. Benedict. It was a point of respect. And I felt a little sorry for him because he didn't command more respect from my fellow patients.

Of course, everyone had a nickname, or almost everyone. The social worker with witch-black hair and dark half-moon sacks under her eyes was Death. The Sunday nurse with the thick brogue, who played Scrabble with us and took us for muffins, was Irish. We called Sylvie, beloved nurse, by her given name. Susan we called Cathy, after the cartoon-strip *Cathy*. The redhead with the leather bracelet was Joan because she wanted to be Joan Jett, and her dark-haired friend was Mona Lisa, because she was always grinning but you could never figure out what she was thinking.

Dr. Benedict's supervisor, Dr. Salt, we predictably called Dr. Pepper. She was unlike any doctor I had ever met, wearing spike heels and low-cut, clingy wraparound dresses like those designed by Diane von Furstenberg, though she was more of a full-figure gal. Her hair was curled into tight ringlets, and she wore lots of carefully applied makeup. Her eyelids looked like a canyon ridge at sunset. She was what my mother referred to as "put together."

Dr. Benedict's supervision required that he meet with Dr. Salt together with his patients throughout the course of the treatment. Salt's office was only slightly larger than Dr. Benedict's. She sat behind the desk and Dr. Benedict and I faced her. For a moment I imagined us as high school kids who had been caught getting high behind the soccer field. Dr. Benedict draped one arm over the clipboard in his lap. I was always desperate to see what the staff were writing about me, imagining I might discover some great truth about myself in their notes, some key or, barring that, some condemnation or invective that would confirm my worst suspicions.

Salt wanted to know what feelings I had formed toward Dr. Benedict. When I failed to respond, she stunned me by asking if I wanted to marry him. *What is she, a mind reader?*

"I guess so," I said, knowing that any denial would be transparent.

"That's healthy," she said.

I looked over at Dr. Benedict's hairy knuckles and that big fat gold band.

"You realize," Dr. Salt continued, "you're going to have to come to terms with your feelings for your previous therapist." She said this as if it could be accomplished as easily as applying hot compresses to a boil.

I didn't answer right away. What did she know about my previous therapist? She leaned forward and rubbed a spot of lipstick off her tooth with her tongue.

"Are you prepared to confront those feelings, Betsy?"

I looked toward the door; a sticker with some emergency procedure was peeling off from the bottom up. I turned back and saw Dr. Benedict writing away.

"Betsy?"

food and loathing

"How am I supposed to do that?"

"Tell us everything. All your thoughts and feelings."

Right, I thought, *the truth will set me free.* Where was that in the medical books?

Dr. Salt said I had reason to be disappointed with Dr. Mizner, and I must talk about my feelings. I shuddered to recall his deep voice chiding me when I called him from the emergency room, or during my last visit: *Call me when your thoughts crystallize.* She said that expressing those feelings was the work at hand. I still didn't understand how therapy was work. I never quite got that concept: sitting and talking about yourself—*hard day.*

My sessions with Dr. Benedict were at 7:30 A.M., three mornings a week. I wasn't sure, but I believed I was Dr. B's first patient. I dreamed of being his first great case. His Anna O. His Wolfman. More likely we resembled two people on a nervous blind date. In the beginning we sat in silence for long stretches of time. It was clear that it was I who would have to break the silence, and I acted as if it were a competition or test of wills, sometimes sitting without saying a word for twenty minutes. Often I had the urge to lean forward in my chair and shout, "Boo!"

Benedict, who was left-handed, curled his hand

around his pen as if he were hiding what he was writing. He wrote constantly, even in the silence. What the hell was he writing? Mizner had never taken so much as a note.

After a couple of months Benedict traded in his Bic for a fountain pen. Suddenly I had lots to say about that, conjecturing who gave it to him, warning him that one day his breast pocket would resemble an inky Rorschach blot. I berated him for using blue ink instead of black, which was infinitely cooler. I told him I knew for a fact that Freud used black ink, though I made that up. He wanted to know why I was so interested, and I said I guessed it was because I was a writer, I liked pens. Some time later I noticed that he had switched to black.

"How come you switched ink? To black?"

Dr. Benedict looked at his pen, as if this were the first he'd heard about it.

"How does it make you feel?"

"Come on, you gotta be kidding. I notice that you've changed your ink and you ask me how it makes me feel. Aren't you going a little too far with this 'how does it make me feel' bullshit?"

"Well, you obviously have strong feelings about it."

"Well, I obviously shamed you into changing your ink, so the question is, 'How does it make *you* feel?'"

"Why did you feel you needed to shame me into it?"

"I didn't need to shame you into anything. You obviously felt you should make a change. Maybe it has nothing to do with me. Maybe the blue ink came with the pen and you were just using it up, for all I know. I just noticed that you finally switched to black. Okay?"

"I think we should stay with this."

"You stay with it," I spat. He seemed truly surprised, even hurt, by my aggression. And I had to wonder why I wanted to destroy this man who was trying so hard to help me.

Dr. Benedict wore the same style khakis, shoes, button-down Oxford shirt (blue or white), and knit tie every day. Though he was always racing down the long corridors like a large jackrabbit as if late for an appointment, he was always on time. He continued to take copious notes in his frenzied handwriting. I loved his rimless glasses. They were probably de rigueur for shrinks in training, but I loved their delicacy. I imagined him peeling them away from his face at the end of a long day and rubbing his tired eyes. I wondered if he told his wife about me.

One day a geriatric patient was brought to our floor for Dr. Benedict to assess. All the interview rooms were in use, so he knelt down next to her wheelchair in the hallway. Name, age, address, do you know where you are, who is the president? The woman stared straight ahead and refused to make eye contact with him. She answered the questions so softly that he had to ask her to speak up a couple of times. A single long braid of beautiful white hair was pinned around her head in what once must have been a perfect bun, only now it drooped off the side of her head.

"Tell me, Mrs. Rosen, who is the president?"

The woman just sat there, nervously flicking an end of the folder with an ancient fingernail so brittle it looked like a chip of mica.

"Can you just tell me who the president is?" Dr. B's voice got a little more forceful.

The woman muttered something indiscernible.

"What was that, Mrs. Rosen?"

"The actor, what's his name, from California."

At that Benedict smiled and stood, made a note. Then he put his hands on her shoulders and began to gently rub, her back and neck visibly relaxing under his touch. I could almost feel it in my own body.

***

Most mornings on the floor were sleepy, drugged, slow to get started. But Wednesdays buzzed like the first cold snap of winter. All of the patients, nursing staff, social workers, and physicians gathered in the day room, where an enormous circle of folding chairs were set up for the community meeting. Afterward, at the staff conference, everyone's privilege status was decided, based on the weeklong staff appraisal as well as on what happened in the meeting. Each week we waited for Dr. More and his staff to emerge from their consultation and for the head nurse to post the list of privileges. We watched the board with all the hope and desperation of a chronic gambler watching the races come in at OTB.

The meeting was officially run by Dr. More, who had conducted my intake interview and who ran the place—though he would have said that it was *our* meeting, that no one person ran it. There was much I wanted to say or ask during that first community meeting, but I felt my body tighten with anxiety.

I had officially stopped speaking in public during a college course on American fiction between the Wars. We had been assigned *Tender Is the Night.* I loved the book so much I read it twice.

"What was Fitzgerald trying to say with the book?" the professor asked the class.

Silence.

"What period was he writing about?"

Watch Out Birds!

Silence.

The professor, her voice growing desperate, asked if we could identify with the story.

No response.

She looped her thumbs in her wide elastic belt and snapped it. "What can you tell me about the main character?" she implored.

My heart was pounding so hard in my chest I felt I would have a heart attack if I didn't answer, yet I remained silent. She turned toward the board and lifted an eraser in her right hand. "Can anyone tell me the main character's name?"

It felt like the end of a nightmare in which I'm trying to call out for help but cannot find my voice. *Dick Diver. Dick Diver.* I wanted to call it out and wake us all, but I sat there. And then our professor did something quite unexpected: she lifted the eraser over her head and flung it into the class. A tall boy in a black leather jacket jumped up to make the catch.

"You're actually awake—how interesting," she said.

The class laughed.

"Now get out of my sight," she said. "And if you haven't done the reading by Wednesday, do me a favor and don't come back."

Everyone gathered their books in their packs and

headed out. I lingered by her desk and finally blurted out that I had loved the book.

She looked up at me and shook her head. "Only now it's too late."

~⊗~

The silence building in that community meeting was combustible. I knew I should jump in, but I sat there thinking about Dick Diver and all the other missed opportunities in classes or at OA meetings, when I had an idea and failed to voice it, or knew I should come to the defense of someone weaker and didn't, all those moments when I just sat there and let the opportunity slip away. I knew then that each of those moments had slowly chipped away at my person, just as regret had shaped those same memories.

Finally, Dr. More took the floor. "This is your meeting, people. You don't need to wait for me to start."

"We weren't waiting for you," Danny muttered under his breath. He was slumped in his chair, eyes downcast, legs extended and crossed at the ankles, and he had his headphones on.

"Would you mind saying that so we could all hear?" Death's voice was low and stern.

Danny didn't move. It wasn't clear whether he was listening to music or just using his headphones as a decoy so he could listen in on people when he appeared to be tuning out.

"Danny, would you please remove your headphones and participate? We all would like to know what you said."

At that Danny flipped the headset back so it settled into place around his neck like a loose collar. "I said I'd rather not listen to all the bullshit here, if you don't mind."

"You seem angry," Death said.

I soon learned that this was a common observation leveled at the patients. *Yes, underneath our Thorazine/lithium/Halcion blanket, we are mad as hell.* What were we supposed to say? *I'm not angry.* Danny started to seethe. I could see his muscles tighten, the vein in his temple go jiggy.

"Do you feel this meeting is 'bullshit'?" Death asked, making quotation marks with her fingers around the offending word.

I wanted to roll my eyes but thought better of it, lest I call attention to myself. I was astonished that the meeting was under way. I had been waiting for an official agenda or some formal remarks from Dr. More. I thought we were going to talk about *something*. It turned out the community meeting wasn't for discussing floor policies, rules, or gripes. It was the Big Event, the Psychological Cock Fight. Showtime. Anything could happen—but that was the point: it was supposed to just happen, not be manufactured. A therapy session writ large. Once the room remained silent for half an hour. I thought my tongue would dry up and rot in my mouth with the pressure of not speaking.

"Danny, if this is bullshit, why do you come?"

"Excuse me? It's required attendance. That's exactly what I mean by your bullshit. You ask me why I come. I don't have a choice. Because if I had a choice, I wouldn't be here. Do I have a choice?" Danny had been a Princeton undergraduate before getting derailed. I didn't know why he was here. Amy told me he tried to gas himself, but I took that as hearsay. More than half of what I had learned about people at the other hospital was wrong. But as Danny argued with Death, I could hear the bright, argumentative pre-law student he once was.

"Is that how all of you feel?" Death opened it up.

Cathy (Susan) chimed in, "That's how I feel." She smiled conspiratorially toward Danny, but he didn't return the smile.

"Let's not take the focus off Danny," Dr. More said gently. Death acknowledged her mistake with a deferential nod in his direction.

She tried again. "Danny, it seems to me that you are

shutting us out with the Walkman and that you have a great deal of anger you need to deal with."

"Duh," Danny nearly spat.

I wondered just then about the intake interview. All the other patients seemed to be here against their will. Had I been duped?

"Danny," Dr. More continued, "you nearly killed yourself less than a month ago. Don't you think you need to understand why?"

"I didn't try to kill myself." Danny was nearly shrieking. "It was an accident." He folded his arms over his chest and dropped his head. I thought he was about to cry when he raised his arm and shook it at Dr. More. "Do you hear? Do you hear me?"

"I hear you, but I don't think it was an accident."

Danny pulled his headphones back over his ears and closed his eyes, refusing to listen.

Dr. More looked at each of us, circling the room as if picking out a suspect in a line-up. His voice was grave. He said that it was natural for us to try and hide what was most painful. As he spoke, it was evident that we were each traveling back in time to the bottle of pills, the razor blade, the gun barrel, the bridge. I imagined Danny sealing off his apartment with towels, turning the gas on, sitting back on the couch wearing his Walkman, much the way he was sitting now.

"I think the fact that we try to cover up our attempts is a good thing," Dr. More continued. "We feel ashamed because the healthy part of ourselves knows that we crossed a line."

"Dr. More," Cathy interrupted, "are they going to put carrots back on the menu?"

A few of us couldn't help but laugh.

"A lot of you are still hiding. You're not going to get better until you can be honest about what happened and why you're here." Dr. More looked up at the clock and cupped his wristwatch. "Okay then, have a good week, everyone. Staff, in the north meeting room for privileges."

Everyone filed out. Danny walked to the picture window and stared out into the white air of late winter. I wanted to say something but didn't. The windows made me think of the construction paper signs we used to make in elementary school to warn the small birds who, mistaking the plate glass windows for air, died mid-flight. "Watch Out Birds!" Like angels, we thought we could save them, keep them from this death, to find another less tragic, less holy.

Watch Out Birds!

My parents came for the family therapy sessions. Death ran these sessions, and I whispered her nickname to my mother before our first meeting.

"Why do they call her that?"

"You'll see." I thought of Death's long, gray-green face, her sharp teeth, her calf-length wool skirts. You could all but imagine the scythe.

When we had all taken our seats, Death introduced herself by her real name. She smiled weakly at each of us. My mother had settled into the one chair with arms, which she gripped. Death started with her.

"Mrs. Lerner," she said. "Do you have any feelings about being here?"

My mother snorted a laugh and looked away. *Any feelings?* I looked over at her—the Ferragamo shoes and belt, the blouse and blazer. Her nails were done, her makeup on, her hair blown. A matching bag hung from the arm of her chair. She was a mannequin of my mother staring off into space.

Death turned to my father, who started explaining how things went wrong when I left Morgan Stanley. How I had gotten two raises in less than a year.

"But that's not why we're here, is it, Mr. Lerner?"

My father looked to me as if I might bail him out. I remained silent.

food and loathing

I was afraid of what Death might say to me, what she might ask me. But she returned to my father. "How do you feel about your daughter being here, Mr. Lerner?"

"Our older daughter is married," my father started. "She's a social worker, and our little one is in high school. She's very bright. Betsy's also very bright."

"But you still haven't told me how you feel about her being here."

My father stammered in response, and I wanted to help him. When my mother first met my father he had a slight stammer. She told me she thought that all he needed was some love to cure his staccato speech. But he continued to stammer, so either he never got the love he needed or a speech impediment is impervious to love. I was caught between the desire to bail him out and the wish to let him trip over his own words.

"I want to know how you feel about Betsy's being here, Mr. Lerner."

"You don't understand, Mrs.— Forgive me, I don't remember your name. Betsy was always bright. We always loved her. We still love her."

My father looked at me. I felt a wave of revulsion.

"Mr. Lerner, I understand that you love your daughter. That is why you're here. And I know that Betsy appreciates your participating. What I'm asking is, can you identify how you feel about her being here?"

It was quiet then, quiet enough to hear the sole of my mother's shoe make a slow circle on the floor.

"How the hell do you think I feel?" My father's tone turned sharp and cynical. His attempts at friendliness had been exhausted. He had been pushed and now he was tired. When his generosity snapped, he suddenly resented everything he had done out of love. I knew not to push my father beyond this point, but Death wasn't afraid of him.

"You sound angry, Mr. Lerner."

"Of course I'm angry. How would you feel if your daughter wound up here? How would you feel?"

"I would feel disappointed and concerned."

"Right, well, that's how my wife and I feel."

"Mrs. Lerner?"

My mother nodded her head in assent.

When they left, I collapsed on my bed. I never went to the dormitory during the day, but that day I was incapable of doing anything else. I cried for a while, wrote in my diary, and slept through dinner. A first.

With each passing week, Death pushed us to confront a variety of what she saw as key issues. We talked about the rivalry between my older sister and me. We talked about the money my father provided and whether there were strings attached. We talked about my parents' offer to buy me an apartment. I insisted that this would only further obligate me, if only emotionally. Death disagreed. She told me I would feel emotionally obligated regardless of whether I accepted financial help or not.

Death was nothing if not pragmatic. I was certain that she had me pegged as a spoiled rich kid and that she would side with my parents, but Death became one of my great allies in the hospital. And after a few months of sessions, in which my mother mostly checked out and my father kept things light, she suddenly turned, put her hands on my shoulders, looked me directly in the eye, and said, "With or without your parents, you are going to get well."

When I found a copy of Janet Malcolm's *Psychoanalysis: The Impossible Profession* in the hospital library, I devoured it. I was especially taken with the idea that analysis ends when, as psychiatrist Aaron Green says, "the patient resolves his transference neurosis—when he finally accepts that the analyst is *not, not, not* going to fulfill the wishes the patient had as a child toward his parents . . .

that he is an adult and must put away childish things. Which is *horribly painful.*" I realized as I read it that I had tried to turn Dr. Mizner into my father and had done the same with Dr. Rostenberg and Dr. More. With Dr. Benedict the dynamic was different because he was closer to me in age and wasn't an authority figure per se, but I was still looking to him to save me. *Oh, to think he changed the color of the ink in his pen for me!*

And then I had all these mommy figures to contend with. All of my negative emotions centered on Adele, the woman who ran the "soft" therapy groups—art therapy, occupational therapy, and so on. She had an eggplant figure and shiny, straight brown hair that I quite admired. Her cloying kindergarten-teacher tone struck me as completely condescending, and within moments of meeting her I determined that she was useless to me in every regard, and I would never let her near me. Yet, like a cat who seeks out the one allergic person in a room, Adele leapt on me. She tried constantly to win my favor, to connect with me, to exact my participation.

During one session of art therapy, we were asked to cut and paste pictures of seascapes. Two student teachers were working with us, and the very sight of them made me sick. You could tell they were a little nervous being around real live mental patients; they wore wide grins and bent their heads this way and that as they handed out art supplies. One was very pretty, very blond, with a denim wraparound skirt. Danny cornered her and flirted like crazy. The other had bad acne scars and wore Birkenstocks that looked like loaves of brown bread. Adele came around to my side of the table and noticed that the boat I had drawn was upside down.

"Are you feeling a little lost at sea today?"

"That's right, Adele," I said, my voice dripping with irony.

"Do you want to talk about it?" she responded with earnest care.

I wanted just then to take the rounded baby scissors we were allowed to use (though even with these a strict scissors count was taken at the end of the art session) and plunge them into her skull. I started to cry, startled by the power of my violence. Adele took this as an invitation to draw near and put her arm around my shoulder. I felt my skin turn hot and shook my head no in response. She squeezed me once more and I shook her off. I put my head on the table and remained that way for the rest of the session.

In my next session with Dr. Benedict, he asked me what had happened in art. I told him how uncomfortable

I felt with the student teachers and their nervous glances. How Danny would have raped one of them if he had had half a chance.

"What about Adele?" he asked.

"What about her?"

"You tell me."

I fell into a silent stupor the way I used to in Mizner's office. I thought about Adele—that voice, the way every sentence ended on an ascending note, those huge hips and crocheted sweaters; how she approached me the first week and asked me about poetry, as if that would be a point in common. The more she wanted me to confide in her, the more I felt I had to push her away. Her love, her care, struck me as unconditional and, even worse, unconsidered. I could only trust someone who distinguished between people, who was discriminating, who could be cruel.

"Doesn't she know how much I hate her?" I finally said. "How could she be such a fool? She actually thought she made an intelligent observation about my upside-down boat. I drew it *because* it was a cliché. Because I knew she would say something stupid. It was like a piece of cheese in a trap and she jumped at it."

"And how did that make you feel?"

"You really want to know? I wanted to stab her in the head with the scissors. I wanted to stab her fuckin' head in."

Dr. Benedict was writing furiously, his eyes a little dilated, or so it seemed. I realized that I might have privileges taken away for this violent admission, but I didn't care. I wanted to rip the place apart brick by brick. I wanted to lift Dr. Benedict in his chair and throw it and him out the window. I imagined him still crouched over his clipboard in midair, writing everything down. I saw Death on her broom screaming by. I saw my hands holding the bloody scissors, the acne-scarred student teacher trying to run away. Finding the door locked from the outside, she'd turn to me, begging for mercy.

Only I am small, standing outside my parents' bedroom. A wolf rocks maniacally in the hallway. I cannot call out.

⁓

Tuesday morning: weigh day. Standing in line brought me back to those fall mornings in the junior high school gymnasium, where our developing bodies were telegraphing our romantic futures. Each week I conspired to wear clothing that weighed the least. I did everything I could to resolve my near-constant constipation before weigh-in, even eating the soggy stewed prunes that were always available in the cafeteria. They reminded me of small animal turds dissolving in their watery juices. Even with all the therapy sessions I attended, nothing was as powerful a compass of my mood or a better indication of my self-worth than the number on the scale. In the hospital I couldn't tell whether I was losing or gaining. It was never more than one or two pounds, but the direction of the scale provided me with an immediate emotional correlative. In college, when I first encountered Descartes, it took me no time to translate his famous dictum into something I could relate to: *I weigh x, therefore I am shit.*

For the two anorectic women on the floor, this ritual was an extreme trial. Sometimes one would flat-out refuse to step on the scale, and an enormous fight would ensue between her and the staff. The other would stand backward on the scale so as not to see her weight, then spend the rest of the week begging each new nurse who came on duty to tell her the number. The worst behavior surrounding food culminated during an evening of sitcoms when one of the anorectics was not allowed to use the bathroom. She insisted that she had to pee, but apparently she had been throwing up again and it was too soon after she had eaten. The orderly on duty had been given strict orders not to let her go until bedtime, when her meal would have been digested. In a hideous struggle with the orderly, she finally wrested herself free and threw up in the closest garbage can.

Listening to these women in group therapy I learned about everything from laxative abuse to swallowing ipecac, which makes you throw up. It also can cause heart failure, and apparently this is what Karen Carpenter died of. *We've only just begun.* I was just a plain old compulsive overeater. For all my self-loathing, I never tried to throw up or take Ex-Lax, never got dangerously thin. In the face of the problems these women had with food (one had false teeth, having ruined her own from too much puking), I felt that my own were surmountable. Sometimes I even managed to let go of the number on the scale, like an age you can't believe you've reached.

The food at the hospital was terrible, but it was still possible to gain weight, especially after weekends, when the patients with passes returned with angel food cakes and brownies and cookies. I rarely partook, as I was still generally a closet eater who never wanted to be seen indulging, lest someone comment, "Do you really need that?" Once, when the only sweet thing around was a walnut brownie, I took it with me into the bathroom, even though I am deathly allergic to nuts, and nibbled around them like a small rodent. Other times I would sneak some forbidden food into my cubby and eat it in the middle of the night. I had officially joined the cacophony of sick motherfuckers.

Then there were the Sunday outings with Irish, the gentle nurse with a lilting brogue and jet-black hair swept up into an enormous cottony pile. She would walk the patients with privileges to the local Twin Donuts to pick up a box of doughnuts and muffins the size of Studebakers. Those muffins were like love melting in your mouth. I always took bran—avoiding the more fattening corn and blueberry, I falsely rationalized. I'd sit in one of the lounge chairs off to the side in the library, where we enjoyed our Sunday diversions. Everything in the library, including the windows, was covered by a thick film of grime. The half-empty shelves were so thick with it you could write your name there, and some of the patients had. Still, a shaft of light always warmed the spot where I liked to retreat and enjoy my muffin in masturbatory privacy. In those months I made my way through a number of books you would never finish unless you were in grad school or locked up, including *Middlemarch, Don Quixote,* and Judith Rossner's *August.*

food and loathing

It was a May morning, and the trees along Riverside Drive looked neon; the dogwood blossoms folded like dinner napkins waiting to be opened. My allergies were making me irritable, and all the best seats at community meeting—that is, away from the staff—had been filled. As she often did, Cathy spoke first and I marveled at how easily she broke the ice, how completely uncensored and unabashed she was, taking up our time with her petty concerns about the menu or designated smoking areas, while the great me sat by silently.

She was the kind of girl who in another setting, say at camp or the playground, would have had no position. A child in a woman's body, she carried a teddy bear with her at all times and smoked menthol cigarettes. Her string-straight hair came down to her coccyx. You could tell she thought her hair was very beautiful, her strong suit, by the way she lovingly brushed it and handled it, but it was dead hair, and made her chubby face and body look all the rounder by contrast. She kept her fingernails long and pointed. Though paper thin, they never broke. Unlike everyone else on the floor, who seemed to be here on sabbatical from a real life, who seemed derailed from some pursuit, she seemed content in the world of daytime television and commercials, of magazines and coupons. She was often alone in the day room watching the roster of afternoon soaps, clipping coupons. What she did with them I will never know. Sometimes she'd busy herself assembling a thousand-piece puzzle of kittens in a basket.

That day, uncharacteristically, she started crying when she spoke. "Everyone hates me," she said, her round face streaked with tears.

Sylvie put her arm around her. "Cathy, did you even consider the possibility that it is you who hates everyone?"

Sylvie's observation struck me as true, and helped explain the hostility and bizarreness of much of Cathy's behavior. It suddenly made perfect sense: Of course she hated everyone. I saw how easily anger could be converted into paranoia.

"What I want to know," I finally blurted, breaking my months-long silence, "what I want to know is whether we're supposed to change or just accept who we are?" I directed my question to Dr. More, for it was his response I wanted. But he pulled a classic maneuver and opened my question up to the group.

"How would some of you answer Betsy's very good question?"

Danny jumped in, for the first time in a long time, and said that it was a little bit of both. This was a classic response on Danny's part—with him everything was on the one hand this, on the other hand that.

Someone else said you can't change unless you accept who you are.

"How are you supposed to accept who you are if you hate who you are?" This from Joan Jett.

"That's a good question." Dr. More looked around the circle. "Anyone?"

My chin started to quiver and I could barely keep back my tears. I had finally spoken, attempting to get some feedback from Dr. More, and all I got were some Hallmark sayings. I thought about all those circles of folding chairs where I had uttered the serenity prayer offered at OA meetings: *God grant me the serenity to accept the things I cannot change, the courage to change the things I can, and the wisdom to know the difference.* I still didn't know the difference.

I looked at the faces of my fellow patients and the doctors, nurses, and social workers. Outside a soft rain had started to fall.

"I want to know what *you* think," I said, facing Dr. More.

"Why are my thoughts any more important than anyone else's?"

"Because they are, because you run this place. This is our one chance to hear what you have to say."

"And you think my thoughts might be more valuable?"

I nodded affirmatively.

"Does anyone else feel that way about what I have to say?"

Danny said that More's relative absence rendered his thoughts less interesting, less worthy. "You're never here. I don't care what you have to say." Danny, reliably, was in complete denial.

"Does anyone else agree?"

A few others chimed in. They saw Dr. More as a benign but distant presence. A classically cold father.

"I feel the opposite," I said, feeling somewhat more composed. I was thinking about my father and how I used to worry the linoleum waiting for his return each night. I did the same as we waited for Dr. More to show up at the community meeting, turning toward the door with anticipation each time it opened. And feeling abject rejection when he was away on holiday or sick.

"I think you're right, Betsy," he started. "I think most of you don't want to admit how much you miss me."

Danny snorted at this suggestion, but I knew it was

true. It wasn't cool to admit it, but I said I wished he would spend more time with us.

Dr. More shook his head in what appeared to be vigorous agreement.

"But you still haven't answered my question," I said. Having discovered that I could talk, I wanted an answer.

"Well," Dr. More said. He was in a different mood now. There was no more ping-ponging my question around the circle. His voice became slow and deliberate, and I settled into my chair as if for the reading of a will.

"The therapy we are doing here is like the work that is done in a laboratory. What counts more than any individual therapist is your capacity to grow. If you are unwilling to share your feelings, then you will never grow. What I think most of you fail to see is that the longer you remain silent, here and with your therapists, the more nails you put in your own coffin, the more dirt you heap upon your own graves. Some of you have lost parents or siblings to suicide. Some of you have tried to kill yourselves, some more than once. You must learn to mourn in order to heal. People who are never able to mourn the dead make their home a mausoleum." As he spoke, I saw the long corridor of our temple where the Wall of the Dead throbbed with the memory of so much loss, people who had led full lives and those, like my little sister, whose lives had not yet begun.

The day after my sister's funeral, my mother took my older sister and me shopping. The late autumn air had a chill, and we needed new winter coats. We were new in town, and the owner of the children's store didn't know our family, hadn't a clue about the tragedy from which we had just emerged. He treated us as he would any mother with two daughters in tow. Once we were properly fitted and the bill paid, he handed us two lollipops.

"We need three," my mother tells me I said.

Nine

Food and Loathing

Mona Lisa made me do it. She had full privileges, to my recently expanded area privileges, which allowed me to go outside the hospital within a ten-block radius. She wanted to see a movie that was playing on the Upper West Side. Normally, she would have gone with her best friend, Ann (Joan Jett), but Ann's privileges had recently been revoked. Over the last few weeks, she had been withdrawing from groups, participating less, acting surly and irritable. She didn't want to play cards, didn't go to Sylvie's Tuesday-night grooming session, where we gave each other manicures. I had no idea what was going on with Ann. When I first arrived, Danny told me she had tried to kill herself with her dad's revolver. Ann's dad was a cop, so when Danny said it, I didn't question him.

Ann acted as if her reduction of privileges was an outrageous miscarriage of justice and complained bitterly to anyone who would listen, even taking the floor at community meeting.

"This is just so fucked up. You people have no idea." She twisted the studded leather bracelet around her wrist as she spoke.

"What is it we have no idea about, Ann? Why don't you tell us?" one of the doctors responded.

There were days when you could see beneath the spiky hair, the black leather, the thunderbolt tattooed on her forearm. You could see a girl so pretty she could have been a *Seventeen* cover model, with her peaches-and-cream complexion, green-blue eyes, and button nose. I imagined Ann at her family dinner table silently moving the food around her plate with a fork while her father stuffed a pork chop into his mouth; Ann in the back seat of her boyfriend's car (she talked about her boyfriend constantly), his taut body sprawled out with Ann on top, riding his hips as if they were a beautiful saddle. I tried to imagine Ann loading her dad's revolver, sticking it in her mouth, her favorite Foreigner song cranked up to ten, "I Want to Know What Love Is."

"You just have no fucking idea who I am." Ann rolled her eyes toward the ceiling, spread her legs, and planted her feet wide. She had a lot of masculine mannerisms and poses. I admired her. I often thought that if I lost some real weight again I would cut off my hair, dye it black, pierce my nose, and assault the world the way the punks of St. Marks Place did with their spikes and safety pins.

The last news story I had followed with any fervor was that of Sid Vicious murdering his girlfriend, Nancy Spungen, in the Chelsea Hotel. The headlines told a story of love and squalor that I yearned to experience. The Chelsea Hotel had a long mythology of starving artists and junkies who would squat there for months, trading art for rent. I used to sit in the lobby and gaze at the enormous paintings that choked the walls. I'd go to the neighboring bar, El Quijote, and smoke my Marlboro Lights while nursing a single Corona with a wedge of lime, reading Camus's diaries, Patti Smith's *Babel*. I had been born too late. Not that I would have been part of the scene. Just getting into Max's Kansas City, with its bouncers and velvet ropes, was an ordeal for me. I dreamed of being one of those girls with kohl-darkened eyes who slipped in and became one with the dance floor. Instead, I'd stand against a wall and let the music wash through me like chemicals. I dreamed of sending myself off on a raft of heroin, sailing away from the girl clutching her bag, making sure her wallet was still there with her dorm card and meal ticket.

"I think Ann's angry." This from Cathy, with a smug half-laugh on her face, amused at her own joke. She clearly thought she would win favor among the patients.

"You think that's funny, fat girl?" Ann snarled back.

Cathy, nervously looking for recognition, started laughing harder out of sheer anxiety. I couldn't stand Cathy, but I was stung by Ann's remark. Even here, life was ultimately reduced to a playground mentality.

As I sat in that meeting, I realized that I wouldn't be staying at the hospital much longer. I wasn't a mental case like Cathy and I wasn't resisting all treatment, like Ann and most of those around me. Ann had been at the hospital for close to a year, and she was still as angry as most people are the day they arrive, still in fierce denial about whatever form her self-destruction took. Mona Lisa had been there two years and none of us knew why, though I began to suspect she was an alcoholic, among other things. Danny had been there a few months more than I, but he showed no signs of progress. The anorectics kept bouncing from our floor to intensive care for tube feeding. And Amy, who first greeted me when I arrived, had sunk into a deeper depression that left her nearly catatonic. No one said anything, but I think she was being sent out for shock therapy. As I looked around the room, I knew that I was making progress.

I had been weaned off all medication for a couple of months. The treatment team believed my depression was responding to therapy. Each week I told Dr. Benedict more and more, and between sessions I wrote everything down and then revealed even those most private thoughts to him, including what had happened with Mizner and about the night I got pregnant. I confessed that I wanted to be on his mind morning, noon, and night. I fantasized that when he came home from work, the first thing his wife would say was "How's Betsy?" as if I were their child. I imagined my grown self stuffed into a high chair, throwing plates and mashed banana around their kitchen. I wanted them to talk about me while they ate their dinner and during commercials while they watched TV. I told Dr. Benedict that I wanted him to be thinking of me when he made love to his wife. I don't know how I had the courage to say all this (maybe I was crazy), but I believed, as they had counseled, that getting well depended on it.

When I agreed to go to the movies with Mona Lisa, I was concerned that I might get caught and jeopardize my privileges. She persuaded me that only the two of us would know; how could we possibly get caught? We took the A train to Columbus Circle, and when we emerged the sky was a drenched blue with just a star or two twinkling above. To the west, the last brushstrokes of a sunset were smudged against the indigo sky. I took all this in as if I were newly arrived from the island of the colorblind. The hospital and its Washington Heights environs was all khaki: every building, every square of linoleum flooring, every patient and orderly was drab. Now I could not stop staring at the people in their bright-colored clothes, with vibrant hair and juicy lips. Everyone looked delicious to me. Where had they been? Where had I been? For the first time since I took myself to the bridge above the highway, I wanted to be back.

After the movie we decided to walk the eight or nine blocks to the next subway station. We still had time before curfew. For once in my life the movie was less interesting to me than the life outside. I was extremely happy to be out among the living, and I must have expressed my enthusiasm in some terribly uncool way because Mona Lisa cut me a look and said, "Calm down, would you?"

"Fuck you."

"What did you say?"

I couldn't say it again. I couldn't believe I had said it at all, especially to her.

"What's your problem?" she pressed.

"I'm just happy. What's your problem?"

"Did you ever think I was upset about Ann?"

I didn't know what Ann had to do with anything just then. My instinct told me Mona Lisa was just dredging up Ann as an excuse for her own nasty behavior. It was hard to know if she ever got honestly upset about anything. She always moved at the same speed, spoke with the same even tone of voice. She was what my mother called a cool customer. Even when Mona Lisa laughed, she just bobbed her head slightly, like a dashboard dog, and let out a small "heh, heh." Right now I didn't care about her trumped-up concern for Ann. Even more, I didn't like being told to calm down. All my life, whether at the family dinner table or with a group of friends, someone would always tell me to calm down when I'd get too exuberant about an idea or take a joke too far. And whenever I heard those words I'd feel the cord yanked out of the wall, the current severed.

Mona Lisa took out a cigarette and lit it. She no longer appeared supremely cool to me. In the wake of her nastiness and outside the context of the hospital, I saw her for what she was: another sad, chronic depressive whose greatest asset was her ability to hide behind a cryptic grin. A small crowd had gathered in a crescent on the next corner, and as we came closer I heard the familiar notes of a song I loved climbing into the air. As we got nearer, the saxophone peeled off a riff from "My Favorite Things." But for the censorious eyes of my friend and my reticence about public displays, I would have thrown my arms into the wind and sung the rest of the song, for I knew every word by heart.

∞

I arrived for my next session with Dr. Benedict bursting with my news of the night before. I told him how hearing the saxophone was like hearing music for the first time, how alive I felt, how beautiful everything looked.

"Were you aware that you were abusing your privileges?" he asked.

"Yeah." The truth is, I didn't care. "The city felt so alive. I felt alive."

"And your friend?"

I realized that I had implicated Mona Lisa in my confession. "But she has full privileges, she can go anywhere in the city."

"Do you think it was right that she compromised your privilege status?"

"I don't see why you're so hung up on that. Isn't what's important the fact that I'm sitting here telling you I actually wanted to live, to get out, to get out of this fucking place?"

"Yes, that's wonderful, but it's through privileges here, and adherence to them, that trust is built with the patients."

Even the word "patients" made me squirm just then. I no longer wanted to be a dull, shadowy figure on a couch in the day room watching a static-filled TV. Couldn't Dr. Benedict just be happy for me? Changing the subject, I relayed how Mona Lisa told me to calm down, and my telling her to fuck herself.

"Why did it bother you so much?"

"I don't know. My mother always told me to calm down, said I was too much. What does that mean, anyway?"

"How were you too much?"

"I don't know. She said I never knew when to stop."

"What would happen?"

"I'd get yelled at for taking things too far. For carrying on. At first everyone would be laughing and getting a bang out of my crazy impressions of our Hebrew school teachers, and then I'd kind of lose control."

"Do you think your mother was afraid of your exuberance?"

"My mother's afraid of anything extreme."

"Do you think you were too much?"

"Maybe too much for my mother."

"Was that the message?"

I turned away from Dr. Benedict. My body felt radioactive. Slow minutes passed in silence.

"Betsy, can you tell me what you're feeling right now?"

I remained quiet. I felt as if the walls were listening.

"Betsy, can you tell me what you're thinking?"

"My sister," I finally said.

"The sister who died?"

"Right."

"Can you tell me about her?"

I couldn't speak. I shook my head no.

"Can you try? I think it's important."

I couldn't look at him. I felt myself shrinking. Dr.

Food and Loathing

Benedict was saying my name, but I was a rock, small enough to fit in his hand.

"Do you think your death wish is tied up with your sister?"

I started to cry, though I didn't know why.

"Do you think you might have been competing with her for attention?"

❧

After the next community meeting, we gathered as usual to wait for changes in our privilege status. I was certain I would get knocked back for the week, and I figured they might limit Mona Lisa's full privileges in some way. For the first time I considered privileges from something other than the patient's point of view. They weren't just little parcels of freedom doled out or withdrawn. Privileges signaled trust, though the behavior that warranted that trust was often unpredictable. Someone doing really well might be bumped back, someone who seemed in awful shape could get increased privileges. That day I saw the method at work: Mona Lisa was restricted to the building, and I was given full privileges. Full! First I called my parents with the good news, then John.

When I emerged from the phone booth, Mona Lisa

stood waiting. She leveled her gaze at me and ever so slightly shook her head in disgust.

Although I had broken the patients' code of silence, I was too excited about my newfound status to feel remorse. It wasn't that I wanted to go anywhere in particular; I was just closer to getting out. And I didn't care if everyone on the floor was mad at me.

That night, when I went to sit down at the spades table, Ann, my usual partner, put her arm up.

"What?" I said, realizing that I was out.

"I'm playing with Kevin tonight."

"Oh." I walked away. Kevin was the worst card player I had ever seen, and his constantly tapping feet drove Ann to distraction. In fact, when I first arrived, I watched her brutally kick him out of a game for driving her mad with his thumping. Fuck them. The spades game was a huge waste of time when I should have been reading. Danny still talked to me when he felt like it, and Cathy saw this as her big chance, now that I was basically on my own. She kept complimenting me and asking if I wanted to brush her hair. *Thanks, anyway.*

Over the next few weeks I began to make my exit plans. I had to look for a place to live when I got out, decide whether or not to return to school. I had to choose some outpatient treatment and find part-time work. Every minute I wasn't in therapy, I was on the phone making appointments, seeing apartments, writing letters to Columbia's Writing Division. I had written to Denis Johnson and told him about being hospitalized. When a letter arrived with his name in square, blocky print in the return address corner, I secreted it away until I could find a few minutes alone. "In a way I envy you," he wrote. "I wish I could shed my skin and start naked and grow right."

❧

I was alone in the TV room. Mona Lisa wasn't feeling well and had gone to bed early. Ann approached to ask for a cigarette and wound up sitting on the couch with me. She said she was happy that I'd be getting out so soon, said she could tell I had a lot going for me. I was surprised by her sudden interest and decided to see if she would open up.

"Ann, what's your story?"

She laughed. "My story, huh? You don't wanna know."

I looked at her and said nothing.

"Okay," she said and started twisting her leather bracelet. I admired the pointy studs. Then, in a sudden gesture, she snapped it off, and there, on the soft underbelly of her wrist were what looked like a tangle of dark branches. I had seen self-inflicted scars and burns before, but never anything like the ones Ann had carved into her skin. I worked hard to conceal my reaction. Tears filled her eyes and she shook her head.

"I really don't know what the fuck is wrong with me."

"You will," I said. "Let them help you."

Ann snorted a laugh and wiped her arm across her face, drying tears and snot in a single gesture. She snapped the bracelet back on.

"I can't believe I'm in this fucking place."

"It's not so bad."

"You really believe in this crap, don't you," she said.

"What choice do you have?"

A few weeks before I was to leave, I spent the morning at the Columbia campus, preregistering for fall classes. On my way back to the hospital, I fell to daydreaming. Without checking the traffic, I stepped onto Broadway nearly in front of an oncoming bus. The charge of those enormous tires an inch from my face sent a shudder of panic through my body. I stepped back onto the curb and looked up the avenue at the whorl of black fumes at the back of the bus. I laughed to myself at the perfect irony.

Food and Loathing

I told Dr. Benedict about my brush with the bus in our next session. He wasn't amused.

"Are you still suicidal?"

I didn't know how to answer. For a moment I worried that if I said yes he could keep me locked up, my life privileges revoked. I decided not to joke about it.

"It's not that I'm not suicidal, it's really that I'm not *not* suicidal."

He cocked his head.

"I don't want to kill myself," I said to clarify. "I think I pretty much know that. Even if I wanted to, I couldn't. I took myself as far as I could go. I don't want to go down that road again."

The self-destructive impulses were quieter now, but never entirely snuffed, like those small orange flames holding vigil at our temple. I understood now that when I turned the bulb beside my sister's name I secretly wished to join her. I still carried an enormous burden of shame for pursuing an end to my life, for having let myself fall so far, and all these negative ideas about myself were still fused with my body image. Food and loathing. No matter how far I had come in deprogramming myself, in intellectually comprehending that who I was and what I weighed were distinct, I could never quite shake the feeling that *if only I were thin. . . .* The work I did with Dr. Benedict had taken me a few steps forward. I no longer believed I belonged in those rooms full of people who labeled themselves anonymous. Even if I had come to New York to be Eleanor Rigby among all the lonely people, I no longer was convinced that I would have to be alone. One diary entry from that time exclaims: *Wore shorts to therapy!* Truly a victory for a girl who believed her thighs were grounds for execution.

⌘

It was a bright, sun-filled morning when Dr. Benedict told me. The leaves had unfurled in a green wave on both sides of the Hudson.

"Betsy," Dr. Benedict said, his voice more grave than usual, "I'm going to be leaving in a month, and we'll need to find someone new for you to work with when you're discharged."

I sensed that he was nervous or uncomfortable telling me, and his unease made me feel momentarily powerful.

"Really," I said. "Do tell."

"I'll be taking a permanent position after my residency ends in June."

"Oh."

"Do you want to know where I'll be going?"

"You mean you'd tell me, not just ask me how I feel about it?"

Dr. Benedict actually smiled at my little joke, and I thought he looked relieved.

"So where are you going?"

"Iowa."

"Iowa," I repeated. I immediately thought of the nationally famous writing program, the Iowa Writers Workshop.

"Impressive," I said. "Congratulations."

"Do you know it?" he said.

"I know the writing program," I said. "I guess you'll get some real writers out there."

"I'll be working at the hospital."

"They have the best writers, you know. I didn't get in there, did I ever tell you that?"

"Joking aside, I would like to know how you feel about this."

"How am I supposed to feel about something I have no say in? Powerless? Does that sound right?"

Dr. Benedict looked down at his pad. I triumphantly noted that for once he wasn't writing anything down.

"You want me to take the notes for today? I don't think it's fair that you get to take all the notes while we're here and I have to write everything down afterward."

Dr. Benedict looked pained, and I was ashamed of my little harangue. He had genuinely tried to help me. He was allowed to pursue his career.

"We should talk about ending. Do you have any questions?"

"Do we start to taper off, is that how it works?" I asked, as if cutting hours were like cutting calories.

"We've had an intense relationship," Dr. B. said. "We have to say goodbye. I don't see the point of playing at goodbye."

"That sounds right," I said. It pleased me, this notion of not playing at goodbye. Parting is real and hard, I told myself, and we were going to deal with it like grown-ups.

I went to the dorm and sobbed into my pillow.

Dr. Benedict had to cancel our next appointment. This had never happened, and when we met again I was concerned. He explained that he had a happy reason to be away. He and his wife had just had a baby. A son.

Oh.

I asked about the name and size and pretended to be excited. I wondered aloud if there was room in the crib for me. HA HA HA.

At the end of the session, I wanted to say something nice, but instead I blurted out, "You know, kids of shrinks are always fucked up."

During our final sessions I accused Dr. Benedict of seeming preoccupied. He insisted that we keep the focus on how I felt. I was aloof and angry most of the time and refused to make eye contact with him.

Though I was petulant in therapy, I was glad to be leaving the hospital, glad to be going back to school. I wondered if something more romantic might be on the horizon with John. My parents had bought me an apartment with a tiny second bedroom, which I planned to line with all my poetry books. I felt ready to leave.

Part of me wanted to run away and avoid my last session with Dr. Benedict. Instead, I arrived a few minutes early and pretended to read from my paperback of *One Hundred Years of Solitude,* but the words were swimming on the page. When Dr. Benedict arrived, I followed him down the hall and watched as he fumbled with his bulky key chain, hoping that the nearness of me was making him nervous. From the moment I sat down, I was aggressive and nasty, which is basically how I'd been acting for the last few sessions, undermining his every effort to help me or be understanding. Finally, he stated the obvious.

"I think you're picking on me because you need me to reject you, make it an all-or-nothing situation." He continued to talk, but I stopped listening. My eyes filled with tears, and I could see Dr. Benedict growing concerned. When he asked me to describe how I was feeling just then, I cried harder. He asked if I felt I hadn't been dealing with our separation and I said I hadn't. But then I started to attack him again, throwing his words back in his face.

"Why don't you tell me how *you* feel? Have you 'separated' from me? Or maybe they teach you how to 'compartmentalize' your feelings. If you have feelings."

"Can you tell me what you need right now?" Dr. Benedict looked pained. I knew he wanted to help me, but I was well into my tantrum.

"What I need? What I need?" I wailed through a wall of tears. "You're leaving me. You're probably glad to get out of this disgusting place. You have your new family." I was barely able to breathe and started looking around for my knapsack, desperate to run out on him before he ran out on me.

"Please stay. Please. Don't you think you've had an effect on me?"

"Right," I said and looked away.

"Betsy, I think we should have another session. I don't want to end this way."

All I could hear was the sound of my name on his lips. It occurred to me that for all our talking, three times a week, we rarely called each other by name. And what is sweeter than hearing your name on the lips of your beloved? Only Dr. Benedict was not my beloved. I realized that all my insolence over the last few weeks was bound up in this moment. I was terrified that I would not be able to tell Dr. Benedict how I felt about him now that it was time to say goodbye. And I was even more afraid that he would retreat from me into some kind of safe professional stance, away from the messy emotions of a polluted girl floating in a pond of her own making.

"What I want to say is that I love you." I fought back tears. " . . . and that I'm grateful for your help." My tears could have filled his small office. Dr. Benedict leaned over with a box of tissues, and I took one. It was momentous, his leaning over with the box, my leaning over to accept, not quite the index fingers of Michelangelo's God and Adam touching, but symbolic nonetheless. I remembered all those sessions with Dr. Mizner, when I refused his Kleenex. There was nothing I tried harder to eradicate in my life than my dependency on others; I believed then that taking one thin sleeve from a box of facial tissues would kill me. I took another tissue now and blew my nose.

"Betsy, I want you to know that you're going to do very well. And as for the love and gratitude, I feel the same. It may be a different kind, but it's the same."

We stood then. My pants were plastered to the back of my legs. We shook hands, and Dr. Benedict touched my arm. I looked at him for the last time, just for a second, before slipping out the door.

Dr. More shook my hand after my last community meeting. When I tried to say how much I had gotten out of the place, he said he knew. For all his bravado, he had a surprisingly weak handshake. Adele and I awkwardly hugged after my last art therapy session. Her hair smelled wonderful, and I was sorry for giving her such a hard time. Sylvie dropped by the dormitory while I was packing.

"We meet again," she said, sitting next to me on the bed.

I smiled, remembering how gentle she had been when I arrived, settling me in.

"You know, you're a winner," she said.

"Yeah, right," I responded. How I had resisted that word from Mizner.

"You are, Betsy. You never wasted a minute in here. You worked very hard. I watched you."

"At what exactly? Navel gazing?" I didn't know why I suddenly felt cynical. I think Sylvie's compliment embarrassed me.

"On confronting yourself and getting well."

I nodded my head.

"You've been a good example, you've given a lot to the other patients."

"Is that why half of them won't talk to me?"

"They aren't shutting you out because of what happened with the privileges, they're jealous they haven't moved as quickly as you."

"Six months! You call six months quickly?"

"For this place, yes."

"Sylvie, can I ask you something? How do you do it every day? Come here, seem so happy and positive?"

"I love what I do."

"Really?"

"Really. There's no secret."

I looked at Sylvie's beautiful skin. I was so close I could see the fine hairs around her jawbone. "I want to thank you," I said, "for everything."

"I'm going to miss you," she said, smoothing her jeans with the heels of her hands and standing up. I watched her tall, slim figure until she turned the corner out of the dormitory.

❧

I returned to Columbia in the fall forty pounds heavier than when I had started a year earlier. Fortunately, most of the people I remembered had graduated, and a new crop of aspiring writers had taken their place in the lounge. Naturally, I believed that a large neon sign over my head advertised the reason for my leave of absence, in case anyone was wondering: *Back from the bin!*

I signed up for a fiction-writing class taught by the man known as Captain Fiction, Gordon Lish. He was notorious for his brutally honest assessments of people's work instead of the usual coddling that went on in graduate school workshops. To get into the class you had to submit a writing sample, and I had turned in a few poems and a short story I had written about Mona Lisa. He told me the story was for shit but the poems had some promise; I could come to the class. It was conducted in a small amphitheater-style room with some five levels of desks in a semicircle. The room was packed, the air abuzz as we awaited Lish's arrival. He was also an editor at Knopf, the distinguished publisher of literary fiction; most of the writers in that room would gladly have traded their kidneys to be published there.

He arrived muttering to himself and plopped his manuscript bag on the desk at the center of the room with a great thud. When he looked up, he acted surprised to see us there. He removed his hat, a safari-like number, examined its interior, and set it down on the desk. He turned to the blackboard and chalked a quote from Aristotle. Then he delivered a monologue about making it, about lasting, about there being one or two people in the room who might actually have a chance as a writer. He talked about stamina, about long-distance races, about making ourselves heard in a world of ten thousand things. His voice was grave and nasal. His hair was silk white. Dressed in khaki from head to toe, he took the persona of a drill sergeant; we, his grunts, were going to get our asses kicked. He would root out the weak. If we wanted to piss with the big dogs, he said, we would learn to hold our water during the four- and five-hour sessions.

Spotlighting one person after another in his fierce gaze, he'd ask us to say who we were and why we were memorable. If you couldn't come up with the right answer fast enough, he'd shine his marvelously seductive attention elsewhere, quickly dismissing the person who failed to charm or indulge the small man at center ring.

He told a handsome fellow in the back row that he was too handsome to be a writer. He told a beautiful woman that she was hiding her talent behind her beauty. He told us about former students whom he published at Knopf, and how they too were once grunts like us. The dangled carrot grew bigger in our collective unconscious.

"You there," he said to a man I had noticed right away, the heaviest man in the class. "What will people remember you for?"

The heavy man shrugged.

"Come on, you know why people will remember you."

I couldn't believe this was happening. In eleventh grade, our mad science teacher once asked us to identify which student would last the longest if we were on a life raft, lost at sea. Before anyone else realized where this question was going, I knew that the fattest boy in the class, Andy Stein, was the target. No one answered, and Andy pretended to look around the room along with the rest of us.

"People, isn't it obvious who would last the longest?" our teacher sneered. "Wouldn't the fattest person in the room, the one with the greatest reservoirs of fat, last the longest?"

We were stunned into silence. Even the kids who had picked on Andy in gym or at the bus stop didn't have the heart to finger him in the classroom.

"It's Andy Stein, people. Andy will live the longest because he has the most fat to draw on. Isn't that right?"

For all the horror I felt toward our teacher just then, and all the pain for Andy's public humiliation, I was also relieved. I had gotten away again. And now, a decade later, in a graduate-level class at Columbia University, I was back in the same boat. Only the teacher wasn't some second-rate high school crank with a mean streak. Rather, he was a renowned publishing professional who had the power to make and break careers.

"You're going to be remembered because you're the fattest guy in the room, isn't that right, sir?" Lish wasn't stopping.

"You don't particularly care how you look, isn't that right?"

The fat man didn't answer.

Lish turned to the board and picked up a piece of chalk.

To his back I blurted, "Everyone cares how they look."

He whipped around, searching the room for the small voice that had challenged him.

"What's that?" he said, finding the general direction of the comment.

"Everyone cares how they look," I said again. The words came out of my mouth, were amplified, had sound, carried.

"Is that right, Miss . . . Miss . . . ?"

"Lerner."

"Is that right, Miss Lerner?"

"That's right," I said. "It doesn't matter what you look like, you still care."

He considered this for a moment, holding the chalk as if it were a cigarette, said "Right," and moved on.

I couldn't believe what had happened. I had spoken up for the fat man. The session wore on, no one else aware of the cosmic shift in the universe that had just occurred.

I stuck with the class, though I never wrote another story.

The fat guy never came back.

⌒

That Thanksgiving my father and I stopped at the cemetery where my sister was buried. The gates were open. An empty Kentucky Fried Chicken box littered the entrance, the white-and-red stripes looking lurid amid the manicured lawns and stately trees that were just beginning to throw their shadows. My father said he wasn't exactly sure where she was buried, then drove right to the spot. When he cut the engine, the world was very quiet. I got out of the car first. The headstone was simple: her name, her birth date, and the date of her death carved in clean lines.

"Twenty-one years," my father said, joining me. He put his arm around my shoulders. "She would be twenty-three."

I couldn't speak. I didn't cry. I wondered how we looked and how it could be that we had never come here before. I tried to think of a prayer for her, but no words came. I imagined her small body, like a bruised fruit, a baby plum. My father started to move away and I tried to hug him, but he was already heading back toward the car. He called himself dumb for forgetting a handkerchief.

I thought of my mother in front of her ironing board, pressing my father's handkerchiefs, making neat piles and laying them in his dresser drawer. Week after week. Month after month. My parents had gone on with their lives somehow. During most of my hospitalization I could barely tolerate the sight of them. I was angry all the time, certain I had done this to myself but convinced they had something to do with it. I was as full of blame as I was of remorse, as full of rage as of love.

They had supported me through the treatment, participating in family therapy, driving into the city each week from Connecticut. But instead of taking in a show and dinner, as was their wont, they were subjected to the scrutiny of the staff and the surliness of their daughter. There were no epiphanies, no moments for the silver screen. At no point did my mother race around the hospital floor like Shirley MacLaine in *Terms of Endearment* and demand drugs for my pain. On the contrary—I used to joke that if I were dying and in great pain my mother would worry that the doctors were too generous with the morphine, that I might get addicted.

When, as a child, I'd complain of having a cold, my mother used to smack the back of her hand against my forehead and declare, "Cool as a cuke." If my mother could not abide illness, could I fault her? If my father took me to the sanctuary of the movies, could I fault him? If we lived as if nothing bad had happened, as if nothing bad could happen, could you fault us?

Dr. Benedict once said that I hadn't been able to trust since the age of four, that I was torn between wanting to be cradled and telling the world to go fuck itself, and that these were opposite sides of the same coin.

Food and Loathing

"What is the coin?" I asked, picturing a fat, gold disk flipping in slow motion.

"Betsy?" his voice a question, "Do you think your sister's death was your parents' fault?"

"No."

"What is your understanding of how it happened?"

"The doctors told my parents she would be all right. They wanted to take her to the hospital, but the doctors said she would be all right. They blame themselves for listening to the doctors, but it wasn't their fault. She didn't get to the hospital in time."

No sooner did those words escape my mouth than the subsequent thought pushed through: *Not like me.*

Epilogue: Starting Tomorrow

No one could see that I had been bell-jarred. In the years following my hospitalization, I managed to rebuild my life. I finished graduate school and embarked on my editorial career. I dated a few men, all the while holding out hope that John and I would get together. I privately marked each anniversary of the day I went in and the day I was released from the hospital. These milestones struck me as profound accomplishments, a testament both to the treatment I had received and to my own will. I still suffered bouts of depression, but I managed to cope, which is all I had ever asked Mizner to help me with. My depression never got in the way of my job; on the contrary, my work was a tonic, and sometimes I laughed recalling occupational therapy sessions in the hospital, hooking rugs. No matter what success I achieved as I advanced in my editorial career, I'd always tell myself, *Nice rug-hooking, Lerner.*

～

After I was released from the hospital, a new drug for depression was introduced. I read with great interest the news of Prozac's transformative effects on people who suffered with chronic depression. Books were written that posited the question I had struggled with since Dr. Parker first wanted to treat me with lithium: Who am I if I am medicated? What is the self? I may not have liked myself, but I was the only self I had. A number of years after Prozac was introduced, after a particularly blue period, I decided to find out for myself and got a prescription for the drug.

One of my professors referred me to Dr. Minot. I was warned that he wasn't the typical shrink, that he would be more interested in my brain than my feelings. Being in treatment with him involved having my brain scanned. The scan was expensive and time-consuming, but I agreed because I was tired of losing weight every spring and summer, only to put it all back on in the fall.

Epilogue: Starting Tomorrow

Tired of torturing myself, of being caught in a never-ending cycle of self-loathing. And tired, too, of the depression always coming back. It was true that I had beaten the high odds of recidivism and evaded the hospital's grasp, but I was curious to see if taking Prozac might break the cycle.

When I returned to find out the results of the scan, Dr. Minot briefly reviewed the contents of my folder. He didn't say anything as his eyes traveled over the chart. Then he snapped the folder shut and looked over the frames of his rectangular bifocals at me. "You are a classic bipolar," he finally said. "Manic-depressive."

My ears went hot. After twenty years the same diagnosis. I remembered Dr. Parker's owl face and bow ties. He had seemed so smug; I didn't believe he knew me at all. I remembered how helpless my parents looked in his office, more like huge stuffed dolls than themselves. Only now did I realize that when Dr. Parker delivered his diagnosis, my parents had already agreed to the medication. I thought of those first few weeks of being on lithium, walking down the painted halls of my high school, dizzy with dry mouth.

Though the technology was still in a developmental stage, Dr. Minot showed me on the scan how the groupings of dots in various lobes of the brain indicated manic depression. In light of his diagnosis, I could recall periods when I needed only four hours of sleep, when I thought I could get a book out of every person I met, when my brain pitched ideas at the rate of a batting machine. Still, I didn't want to believe I was manic-depressive. After all, I had never streaked through Times Square, never squandered vast amounts of money on some insane scheme.

When I explained that the lithium I took as a teen had made me feel like a zombie, Dr. Minot did the math and figured that the dose I probably had been given in 1975 would have had that effect.

"It was the right medication," he said, "the wrong dosage."

He was absolutely certain I needed lithium. He would find just the right dosage to allow me to function creatively—he worked with a lot of creative people. He didn't just medicate by the numbers, he said. He promised me we'd get it right.

When I asked about Prozac, he said he would add a little to the lithium to help me out of this depression.

I agreed to take the medication, but only on the condition that I could stop as soon as I felt better. Minot discouraged this approach. I couldn't understand why I should stay on the lithium once I was feeling better.

The amount of Prozac he prescribed, along with the

lithium, was so small I had to take it in liquid form with an eyedropper. Within weeks I was bouncing out of bed at 5:00 A.M., hitting the pool by 6:00, and at my desk with a double cappuccino by 7:45. When most of my colleagues arrived, between 9:00 and 9:30, I had usually done a whole day's work, my body throbbing along with the steel heart inside my Selectric. Long editorial letters peeled from my fingers. We thrummed. We made beautiful music.

The other telltale sign that I was elevating came in the form of a backless navy blue dress. The American Booksellers Convention was held in New York that year, and there were parties every night. If you were so inclined, it was not very hard to get laid, especially if you wore a backless dress to the Palladium. I slept with two different men that weekend, a writer and a sales rep. I walked through the convention halls feeling as if a spotlight was on me. My brain was as busy with mental activity as the hive inside the entire convention center. My skin buzzed. At each booth, people were talking, schmoozing, looking at books, wondering when they would get lunch, where the bathrooms were. They had no idea I was on fire.

And then I hit the trifecta. In mid-July three things happened on the same day: I won an editorial fellowship to study in London; a publisher I had dreamed of working for offered me a job as a full editor; and, completely out of the blue, without any warning, John called and invited me for a weekend away camping. Just us.

My leg was jiggling and I was talking a mile a minute when I went back for a follow-up appointment with Dr. Minot. He said I should stop taking the Prozac immediately. Even though I couldn't slow down, I said I liked how I was feeling. My brain was racing, I couldn't wait for street lights to change or people to finish their sentences, but I was getting *a lot* done. I asked Minot if I could take a little less Prozac, but he said it was making me manic and I had to stop taking it altogether. He wanted me to stay on the lithium to stabilize me. The way I figured it, my weight was down, my mood was up, I had another promotion, and John and I were getting serious; I threw the medication in the garbage.

John and I moved in together at the end of September, and by December we were engaged. Throughout this period I was too high on the happiness and excitement of being with him to fall prey to my usual autumn blues. I did not gain weight. I did not get depressed. On the contrary, I was flying. I'd still sneak a piece of pizza on the way home from work now and then or throw myself into the nearest deli and devour a black-and-white for old times' sake. But mostly I was holding my own. Swimming and working out. The bridal waistline was happening. I was doing well in a new job. The demons seemed to have shrunk to the size of miniature trolls. They still mocked me, however, wanted to know if I really believed this was going to last.

⁂

Depression returned as reliably as a flock of migrating birds during the first fall of our marriage. It didn't make any sense to me. I had what I wanted most. Still, I grew heavier, thicker, more reclusive. My backless blue dress was sequestered in the far reaches of the closet. No one at work suspected that behind my empathic demeanor I wanted to kill myself. Or that I slept through weekends, didn't wash or get dressed, let the phone ring and ring the way I used to. John grew concerned, begged me to go back to Dr. Minot. John was the only person who had witnessed my suicidal depression before, the only one who had loved me through thick and thin. Now he was asking me to get help before it grew worse.

Dr. Minot wasn't surprised to see me. He said that manic depression was a progressive illness, that without medication each episode of depression would be worse. He also thought that my manic episode on Prozac might be a preview of further manic episodes. I asked him about taking one of the Prozac cousins or any other medication that might work for me. I still didn't want to take lithium.

"Betsy," he asked, "what is this resistance? Lithium will help you."

I couldn't believe that I didn't have a choice. No matter how often I hit the same wall, I believed that I was capable of changing by myself, that any indulgence or self-control was a matter of my will.

"The label *manic-depressive* scares me," I finally said.

"You should be happy that I can treat you. You can be stable for the rest of your life. Not everyone is so easy to treat."

Easy to treat. I had to laugh. I had spent six months in a hospital under the supervision of god knows how many doctors, and no one had even mentioned manic depression.

"Easy to treat if I take lithium, you mean?"

"Yes, of course."

"I just never wanted to be, I know this sounds stupid, really sick. I mean, in a way I should feel relieved because it explains a lot, but I always thought I would have a choice."

"You really don't have a choice." Dr. Minot said and

tossed my chart on a big messy pile of manila folders, signaling that he had nothing more to say. I looked at the pile and wondered if I was just the sum of my brain scan, little dots clustered in my frontal lobe. Is that where the poems came from? The desire to destroy myself? I noticed his pencil cup, stuffed with pens from pharmaceutical companies. I looked at his bookcase and noticed matching portraits of a son and a daughter. I was sure they were older now, that these two pictures were from a different era in his children's lives. My dad had a picture like that on his desk, a photo of me at eleven in a plaid jumper with a white blouse, my hair held down with a barrette after a disastrous hair-cutting experiment I had performed on my bangs. But I am smiling, secure that I am a bright child and that my parents love me, especially my father, whom I take after. I wonder what he makes of that picture now when he goes to work, if he even sees it. Maybe it's just part of the scenery.

Dr. Minot was waiting for me to agree to the medication. This last depression had scared me. It had come on so quickly, not like the gradual wool-gathering in my brain I had known before. I knew Minot was right—I couldn't risk another depression like that. Why was I resisting? I slowly nodded my head, more in defeat than in agreement.

"So you agree?" he gently prodded.

"Yes," I said, and he began filling out the prescription on his white pad.

⸎

When I got pregnant two years later, I went off my medication for the duration, under Dr. Minot's continued supervision. He explained that my moods would be protected by the high levels of hormones pumping through my body as a result of the pregnancy. Not only was I protected, I was boosted. During the summer my usual hypomania (as Dr. Minot described it) was assisted by the hormone boost and brought on a burst of activity. In one swoop, I wrote a book proposal I had been wanting to do for years. I painted a dresser, furnished the nursery in bright primary colors.

I was growing enormous, but for the first time in my life I didn't care. I was like the Blimp hovering over Manhattan. My doctor let me weigh myself at the office visits and report my weight to the nurse. Invariably, the patient before me left the balances in place along the notched arm of the scale: 120, 135, 114. After my turn I'd swat the weights back to the low end like a typewriter return, lest anyone see my weight. I also lied to the nurse, cutting a pound or two off my weight at first. Toward the end I was lying by a full fifteen pounds. When my mother stopped in at my office during my eighth month, she took one look at me and said, "Can't they give you a diuretic or something?"

By the end of the pregnancy I had lost all control, devouring a plate of onion rings the size of bracelets when my work friends took me out to celebrate. I ate two pieces of chocolate cake with buttercream frosting at the shower. Never before would I have eaten these forbidden and fattening foods in front of anyone. Somehow the pregnancy gave me license. Every night at 9:45 I'd head for the Häagen-Dazs, fifteen minutes before the 10:00 closing. This was the dead of winter and it was late at night, at least for the suburbs; I must have looked like a crazed, obese cuckoo bursting through the doors for two scoops of mocha chip.

I gained sixty pounds. The baby weighed six pounds, eight ounces at birth. A peanut. When the doctor came by to check on me after the delivery, I remarked on how small she was.

"She isn't that small," my doctor commented.

"I guess I thought she'd weigh more, given how much weight I put on."

"What did you think you'd have, a twenty-pound baby?"

food and loathing

In the first years of my daughter's life, I joined Weight Watchers so often that I started registering under different names. My favorite alias was Sheila Levine, for the suicidal heroine of Gail Parent's novel *Sheila Levine Is Dead and Living in New York*. As the novel begins, Sheila and most of the heavy women on the Upper East Side have just discovered that the shakes a vendor is selling contain more than 250 calories instead of 70, as advertised. "Who would want to live in such a world?" Sheila cries.

At my first meeting, I was feeling totally bloated and self-conscious, with two boxes of Weight Watchers low-calorie chocolate bars in my lap. The leader, a spry redhead with a great smoky voice, welcomed us. She smiled and asked if we knew why we were there. People raised their hands and offered the usual responses: to lose weight, to get healthy, to learn better eating habits, to find support. The leader jotted all these down with her thick, squeaky marker on the huge pad leaning against an easel.

"Why else?" She scrutinized our faces, and I tried not to look away.

No one responded.

Epilogue: Starting Tomorrow

"Because," she said and smiled, looking directly at me, "today is the first day of the rest of your life."

A poster was fixed on the bulletin board of my seventh-grade homeroom class. The background was neon-green. A neon-pink flower floated toward the top, and along the stem of the flower those same words danced like leaves: *Today is the first day of the rest of your life.*

Not my life.

Not in the seventh grade, not now.

Intellectually, I've come to understand that struggling with weight and food is about love, sex, power, fear, control, father, mother, society. I get that. I understand that addiction to food is the ritual I've learned over a lifetime to cope with, well, everything. And that the deeper addiction is to self-loathing. And yet, somehow, no amount of self-awareness can defend against a bag of my daughter's Pepperidge Farm Goldfish, which I can inhale at Olympic speeds, leaving my chest covered with a fine dusting of bright orange powder.

The first day of the rest of my life is still somewhere in the future. And I still approach every major event as if it were a new target for reaching my goal weight. The first thing I recall about any rite of passage is not what the experience meant, but what I weighed (which was always the greater indicator of how I felt). A high school friend's father once said that losing weight was merely a matter of vanity. Thin people, he said, were more vain and cared more about their looks. The comment has stayed with me. I've searched my soul and I promise you: I'm vain. I'm Carly Simon vain. If it were just about vanity, I'd be Kate Moss.

And yet I don't know anything more plaintive, false, or deluded than the dieter's lament: starting tomorrow. In my case, it took a lifetime of tomorrows struggling with the scale and severe mood swings before I was accurately diagnosed and properly treated. In the seven-plus years that I have stayed on lithium, I have realized that all my fears about the medication were unfounded. In fact, I am more myself now than when I was periodically checking out, either enveloped by my food addiction or under the thumb of depression. While I haven't gotten thin or become Mary Sunshine, I have learned to manage the fluctuations of food and mood. Oddly, there are times when I miss my illness, when being a good citizen is wearying, when I crave the bedcovers as much as the high-octane energy the spring solstice used to bring, when I resent the three salmon-colored pills I have to swallow every night, reminding me that my stability and respite from this illness is dependent on medicine. People say, you wouldn't feel bad about taking medication if you had a kidney problem, why should you feel bad about taking a drug for mental illness? Why? Because there's a stigma attached to any mental problem. And the stigma of weight is even worse.

Every three months I have a blood test and see Dr. Minot. He makes sure the level of medication in my blood isn't toxic. Then we talk for twenty minutes or so about how I'm doing. I can tell he is proud that he's helped me stabilize and what that stability has brought into my life: my marriage, my career, a return to writing, and, most of all, my ability to be present for my daughter; I haven't lost a single day to depression since her birth.

During one of our sessions Dr. Minot indicated that he thought the hospital doctors didn't know what they were doing. There was no reason for me to stay so long; all I needed was lithium.

"Don't you think it was beneficial in some ways?" I asked him.

When Minot shook his head and averted his eyes from me to my chart, I could tell he was thinking: *What a waste.*

I knew he wasn't wrong. I had lost a lot more than the time. Still, I couldn't completely share his view. What happened there had been real.

food and loathing

∞

When I take our daughter for her four-year-old checkup, she is weighed and measured. The doctor examines her, jokes with her, assures me that she is healthy in every way. She asks if I have any questions, and we talk about preschool. And then I tell her that I have one more thing on my mind. The doctor looks at me, waiting, and when I see that my daughter is preoccupied with a crayon, I say, in hushed tones, "Her weight."

"What about it?"

"What exactly do these percentiles mean for weight?"

"She's average. Along a continuum she falls right in the middle. Why?"

"I'm concerned about a potential weight problem. I don't want to be neurotic about it, but it's on my mind."

The doctor sits down and asks why. I tell her that I've had eating problems my whole life.

"Anorexia?" she asks.

"No, just compulsive eating," I say, feeling that usual sharp pain. Unbelievably, I still think of anorexia as the desirable, saintlike disorder, while overeating and getting fat is for slobs.

"You don't look it."

I blanch at this observation. "Well, it's not just me,

it's my family. There's a history of obesity, and my husband's family is also heavy."

"Well, I'm glad you brought it up, then. We'll keep watch. And I'll let you know if I see any problem. For now, just make sure that she gets a range of foods from all the various food groups, and try to be as active as you can as a family. You don't have anything to worry about right now. She's perfectly normal."

I'm nodding as she's saying all this, nearly crying. The sensitivity of the issue is almost too much for me to bear. I look over at my daughter, busy coloring a picture on the thin paper covering the examination table. She hasn't given any thought to her thighs or her belly. The doctor shakes my hand and I feel that she has heard me, respects my concerns. Doesn't think I'm crazy. After she leaves the room, a deep sob forces its way out of my throat. And the tears I have been fighting cascade down my face.

"Mommy, what's wrong?" A cloud of fear crosses my girl's small face. "Are you crying?"

I wipe away the tears and hug her.

"I'm fine, monkey. I just needed that hug."

"Are you sad?"

"Nope, I'm happy," I say, lifting her into my arms and heading out.

"Why did you cry?"

"Because the doctor told me you were perfect, as if I didn't know."

"But why did you cry?"

"Sometimes you cry when you're happy, too."

"You do?" she says, as if this were the strangest concept imaginable.

I thought then of a linoleum print I had made when I was eight years old at an arts camp. I had spent half the summer carving two faces into my square of linoleum, two faces side by side, happy and sad, smile and frown. And then I printed it, carefully pulling the roller of ink across the linoleum. I loved the sticky, tacky texture of the ink as it spread, loved pressing the block to the paper and lifting it to reveal the faces. I made three prints. One red, one blue, and one a mixture of the two. I wonder if even then, as a little girl, I experienced life on the poles. If my happiness and sadness mixed together like those two great swirls of paint.

"But you're happy now?" my daughter asks again, just to be sure.

I squeeze her strong little body.

"So happy," I say.

Acknowledgments

Whoever said you should never work with your friends never met Henry Dunow. His friendship and representation have both been extended with sensitivity, generosity, and his great humor. Early drafts were read by my sisters Nina Palmer and Gail Lerner, both of whom offered encouragement. Rosemary Mahoney was unerring and exacting in her assessment. Her insights remain invaluable to me, her gloss on the use of tense fondly remembered. I am indebted, once again, to Peg Anderson, whose copyediting is an art form. To the people at Simon & Schuster who took me in and took this on, I am deeply grateful: especially to David Rosenthal, to my superb editor Denise Roy, and her assistant, Tara Parsons. Thanks also go to Victoria Meyer and Aileen Boyle. And to Marcella Berger and Marie Florio, who knew me when. I also want to thank Paul Giorgianni, Francis Mas, and Lynne Reitman. I remain indebted to my parents, Roz and Howard Lerner, for their constant love and support. To my daughter, Raffaella Sweet, who gives me life. And always, always to John, who never let me forget that I was a writer.